Leaning on God's Hope

Leaning on God's Hope

on

God's Hope

Moving from Grief to Gratitude

JAMIE TIDD

with ANN BYLE

credo
house publishers

Published in the United States by Credo House Publishers,
a division of Credo Communications, LLC, Grand Rapids, Michigan
credohousepublishers.com

ISBN: 978-1-62586-154-2

Cover and interior design by Frank Gutbrod
Editing by Elizabeth Banks

Printed in the United States of America
First edition

Contents

Foreword

Sometimes you meet someone and you know there is a greater purpose in your meeting than is obvious in the moment. This was my experience when I first met Jamie. We met each other through a mutual friend. Her outgoing, warm personality instantly connected with me. I knew Jamie had been through some very challenging circumstances in her life. My pastor's heart wanted to come alongside and encourage her. That was one of the reasons I wanted to perform the wedding ceremony when she chose to get married. I recall that day seeing her smile. I knew she was finding so much joy in having all her family around. Little did any of us know that shortly after this joyful day, the family would experience unspeakable heartache. As you read Jamie's story, I hope and believe her words and wisdom will be an encouragement to anyone who has dealt with, or is currently dealing with, unpredictable pain and loss.

Recently I found myself in another situation where Jamie impacted my life. We had a mutual friend, Bob Geurink, who lost his life in a tragic accident. Moments after this tragedy occurred, we were both at the scene. I remember vividly how Jamie brought a comforting spirit to the Geurink family that no one else could have brought in that moment. Her personal experience of growing in Christ through her past was reflected beautifully. Her gentle spirit, kindness, thoughtful words, and appropriate silence blended together to bring a Christlike peacefulness in the family's trials. God is using her in ways she doesn't even understand.

I pray and trust that as she has poured out her life on these pages you will experience the same peace and serenity through Christ. I am so thankful Jamie is willing to extend part of her soul to the pages of this book in "hope" of bringing encouragement to others. It is who Jamie is. I am so proud to call her my friend.

Dan Seaborn
President and Founder
Winning At Home, Inc.

Introduction

Leaning on God's Hope has been a labor of love both for myself and for you, my reader. Writing it brought me joy as I remembered God's leading and the many signs of his love through the years. My hope is that this book helps you, too, as you reflect on your own story.

Everyone faces difficult circumstances in their lives. Perhaps you've faced terrible tragedy. Or a broken marriage. Or difficult health issues. Troubled relationships. Prodigal children. Mental illness. Hope can be difficult to find in whatever circumstances you face.

I pray that you find hope in these pages as you read my story and as you engage with it. Reflection Questions are designed to help you dig deeper into your feelings, beliefs, and thoughts about your circumstances and about God. Some will be difficult to answer without prayer and time to reflect, but please use the space following each question to at least start thinking through your answers.

The Hope Reflection section in each chapter is loosely based on one of the Reflection Questions. Each short devotional digs deeper into what God has shown me as I have traveled through the events of my life, and with the prayer at the end of each chapter I offer my heartfelt plea to God on your behalf. I hope you use the extra journaling space to begin telling your story, to write out your own prayers, or to investigate further your thoughts on the questions or the chapter itself.

This isn't an easy book to read, at least parts of it aren't. It's never easy to read about the dissolution of a marriage or the loss of children. But it's the story God gave me and my family, a story that he has used to glorify himself, and a story that I pray helps others see the goodness of God. I'm praying for you, my readers, that you will begin to see God's hope in your own story.

For God's glory,

Jamie Tidd

CHAPTER ONE

A Mother's Nightmare

"*A whole stack of memories never equals one little hope.*"

—CHARLES M. SCHULZ

I woke up feeling like something was out of place. I had no reason to feel this way, but my senses were on high alert that snowy morning in January 2007. I remained on alert as I waited for my ex-husband and three of our children to arrive at my home. They would have already dropped off my oldest son Zachary, thirteen, at school after the night spent with their dad.

The middle two boys—Jordan, age ten, and Spencer, age eight—would catch the bus from my house, then I would take our youngest, Emma, four, to preschool. It was the juggling act of divorced parents sharing custody of the children we loved.

This day, however, it was after eight in the morning and no one had arrived. Typically, they arrived between 7:45 and 7:55 a.m., but it was snowy outside so maybe they were delayed. I called my ex-husband, Curt Boeve, but he didn't answer. I called my husband, Dave, and he said an accident had shut down the highway they traveled and had likely delayed their arrival. I called a friend and asked her to pray because I sensed something was wrong. I called my former mother-in-law, but she didn't know anything. I called the school and asked the school secretary if she had seen my Zach at school. I called and called and called, but no one had answers.

Finally, at eight thirty, someone called me.

"This is the Holland Police Department. Is this Jamie Tidd?"

I said yes, and he followed with several confirmation questions. At this point I was pacing back and forth in a near panic, wanting answers but afraid to ask. The officer finally told me that my former husband had been in an automobile accident and there were injuries to our children. Could I get to Holland Hospital right away?

"Are you alone?" he said. "I'm sending a police cruiser to pick you up because I don't want you to drive alone. It will be there in fifteen minutes or so."

I was immediately on the phone again, panicked but trying to stay calm. I called my husband, Dave, and told him to meet me at the hospital. I called my former mother-in-law, Sharon, back, and she answered the phone sobbing.

"Jamie, don't you know?" she sobbed when I asked her for information about the accident I knew had occurred. We both sobbed as she told me that Curt and Zachary had been killed instantly, a semi-tractor trailer had pulled out in front of the van my family was in and collided, the other three children were on the way to the hospital. "I didn't want to be the one to tell you," she cried.

How does any mother take this news? I was beside myself, panic and fear and grief all balled up in my head and heart. I called Dave back to tell him, then I called my dad, Jim Carl.

"Dad, Zach and Curt have been killed in a car accident and we need to get to the hospital," I cried out to him. He didn't understand and still didn't understand with a second telling. After I told him the third time, I fell to the floor and began screaming.

Dave's parents, Carl and Ruth Tidd, were on the way to be with me after Dave called to tell them. They told me later that as they pulled up to the house, they could hear my screams from outside. They rushed inside in time to answer another call from the police department asking to confirm my address.

"We'll be taking her to the hospital," my mother-in-law said quickly. That drive felt like a slow-motion movie inhabited by people I didn't know. How could this be happening, I wondered.

When we pulled up, a lady waiting at the door asked my name. She clearly knew exactly who I was as she led me to the automatic double doors. The hallway was lined with thirty to forty people, all of whom I knew. Why were they hugging me and crying, acting as if they knew what was going on when I didn't? A doctor appeared and drew me to a quiet section of the emergency room.

"Your son and your ex-husband were killed instantly; they didn't suffer," he said. In my head I was asking why he was telling me this again; I already knew they were gone and I didn't want to hear it again. My mind whirled with these kinds of disjointed thoughts as I fought to keep what little control I had left.

"Spencer and Emma have very severe head injuries and were airlifted to a larger hospital forty-five minutes away in Grand Rapids. Your son Jordan is in a room down the hall, waiting for an ambulance to take him to Grand Rapids. Would you like to see him?"

What a silly question. As we walked toward my injured boy, the doctor stopped me with a hand on my arm.

"I know you've had some very tragic news, but I need you to be as calm as you can. Jordan has no idea what has taken place," said the doctor, who had probably had this conversation many times. "He's in a neck brace so he can't move his head, and he has multiple lacerations so there is a lot of blood. Do the best you can with what you're going to see."

I wondered how bad it could be if my son was still alive, but as I entered the room I realized that nothing had prepared me for seeing my little boy. My knees started to buckle and I began to sob, even as Dave caught me.

"Hi, Mom," he said. "What happened? Where's Daddy?"

I could only look to the doctor amid my sobs. He told Jordan everything was okay, that he had been in an accident, and that his dad was down the hallway. Jordan seemed fine with that explanation. We had no others at that point as we reassured our boy that we would be right behind him on the way to Grand Rapids.

Soon the ambulance came to take Jordan, along with a cadre of victim rights advocates who would transport us and any other family members to Grand Rapids. What a godsend, because none of us could have driven the thirty miles on our own.

When we arrived, the barrage of information began again. My four-year-old princess, Emma, was in surgery to see if they could stop the swelling and bleeding in her brain. Spencer was in the intensive care unit (ICU), with a traumatic brain injury (TBI), and only time would reveal how extensive his injuries were. The swelling in his brain would reach a peak likely within the next forty-eight hours, he was unconscious so was placed into a medically induced coma. Medical personnel told us that when the pressure in his brain reached 20, they would take him into surgery to relieve it by performing a craniotomy. That first night his pressure was at 19.5.

When Emma came out of surgery, the doctors called us into a small conference room. My mind swirled as they told us there was nothing else they could do medically. Her injuries were so severe that she would likely not live;

a brain wave test done later during the night revealed no activity. We were eventually faced with the decision of whether to donate any or all of her organs to Gift of Life.

I never would have believed that at age thirty-six I would be faced with making life-and-death decisions for not one, but two of my precious children, with the possibility of having to do the same thing for the third. It was my, and any mother's, worst nightmare. When I wasn't in one of their rooms—two were across the hall from each other, one a couple of floors up—I was in a conference room talking to doctors or reliving the events over and over to friends and family who came to visit. I was physically and mentally exhausted, unable to shed even one more tear. The numbness was both welcome and excruciating at the same time. I needed to feel and even wanted to feel all of the emotions that swirled around me, but I also wanted to keep them at bay because by doing so I wouldn't have to face the deaths of my beloved children.

We spent that night in a hospitality house attached to the hospital. They had asked us to stay close, but also urged us to get away if only for a few hours. It was so hard to leave, but I recognized the wisdom of what they said. I curled up in a ball on the bed, feeling Dave curl up next to me. I burst into tears yet again. This was the first time we'd been alone all day, finally fully grasping what we were facing and the long road ahead. I longed to see Zachary one more time, to study his features and touch him just once. He'd called me that morning, a rare occurrence on a busy school day. I remembered his voice, and yearned to hear it again.

I prayed, "Why God? Why? My lifelong dream was to be a mom and you gave me four beautiful children, but now you're taking them away? Why?" I finally fell asleep out of sheer exhaustion.

I jerked awake to a room filled with bright light. I thought I was dreaming and remember rubbing my eyes, but the bright light remained. Dave was asleep, but not me. I felt like I was completely out of my body, yet anchored to the bed. I could see a figure in the distance, moving closer to me. Soon I recognized my Zach! Was it really him? Tears rolled down my cheeks as I couldn't stop smiling. I felt such peace.

I started to put a foot on the floor but noticed he had stopped walking toward me. He had a huge smile on his face and he was waving his right hand as if to say, "Hi, Mom! I'm okay." I wanted so badly to hold him, but as I reached for him he moved farther away. I sat on the edge of the bed and tried to make sense of seeing Zach. As I stared at him, I realized what looked like a pane of glass separated us. I believe it was a separation between heaven and earth. The second I realized this, the room went dark.

God had given me exactly what I needed—a glimpse of my healthy and happy eldest son. It was the first glimpse of hope I'd seen in these horrific circumstances, but a hope I didn't recognize until sometime later.

> *Dear brothers and sisters, when troubles of any kind come your way, consider it an opportunity for great joy. For you know that when your faith is tested, your endurance has a chance to grow.*
> —James 1:2–3 (NLT)

Reflection Questions

1. Have you had times when you sensed something was wrong? How did that feel? What happened?

2. What difficult things have you faced in your life? How did you feel God's presence through them? How are you still dealing with these events?

3. How do you process losses in your life? What could you do to be healthier regarding loss?

4. Have you experienced seeing a vision of a loved one who has died? What did that experience mean to you?

5. As you look back, what glimmers of hope do you see as you faced difficult circumstances?

Hope Reflection

Everyone processes loss differently. Yet grief needs to be shared, so I encourage you to talk through it.

Loss causes pain that no words can describe, though it's pretty accurate to say that it feels like your heart is being ripped out of your chest. The gaping hole that's left can be closed only by the world's greatest surgeon, Jesus Christ. You would head to the emergency room immediately if you had a large hole in your body, and you would clean and take care of that wound to prevent infection. With grief, Satan is the infection that loves to destroy.

Don't try to fix the wound yourself because it can't be done. Let God stitch up the hole in your heart left by grief, slowly and in his timing with the hope he promises and the life he will give back to you as you allow him into your life.

Journal

_____

_____

_____

_____

_____

_____

_____

_____

_____

_____

_____

_____

_____

_____

_____

_____

_____

_____

_____

_____

_____

_____

_____

Prayer

Father God, our hearts have some pretty big wounds. Yet we thank you for being the God who sees and who will satisfy our needs with good things. When bitterness overcomes us, grant us the strength to turn away from the enemy's lies and turn to you instead. May our souls find peace and rest in you. In Jesus' name, Amen.

CHAPTER TWO

Blind Faith

*"At the end of the day, we must go forward with hope
and not backward by fear and division."*

—JESSE JACKSON

*S*hared custody of our four children had never been part of the happily-ever-after plan for my life. Curt Boeve and I met in the fall of his senior year and my sophomore year at West Ottawa High School in West Michigan, and I thought I'd met the man of my dreams. We spent every moment possible together during his final year of high school, attending many school events with me proudly on the arm of a handsome senior.

He went off to college, but he came home every weekend so we wouldn't be apart for longer than a few days at a time. I thought we were in love, so I was devastated when he said he needed to have a break over the summer; we'd been dating for several years by then and I didn't know how to not be part of his life. That summer break lasted a month. We were back together, though that was more likely because of the comfortableness of our relationship than our moving forward in it.

My dream had always been to be a mom. I wasn't that little girl who dreamed of going off to college, holding that high-powered executive job, or climbing the corporate ladder. I just wanted to stay home and have babies. After high school, with no marriage looming with Curt and him still in college, I enrolled in cosmetology school. It was an amazing experience! All of my friends there had long-term boyfriends, and we loved to exchange recipes, talk about weddings, and dream about a future that included marriage and kids. I always told them I wanted six kids as we giggled and laughed between breaks in learning to color, cut, and style hair.

I have only one sibling—an older brother named Scott—but I always wished for more. I bugged my parents about adding more kids, but they were adamant. My dad had eight siblings with him landing right in the middle at number five, and my mom was the oldest of six. Perhaps that's the reason they both wanted fewer children, despite raising us as Catholics.

We attended Mass every Sunday morning, along with Sunday school, and catechism on Wednesday nights. My parents did a great job instilling their faith and values into my brother and me, as well as what that faith meant to them. I don't remember talking openly about our Catholic faith, but we knew the rituals that were repeated weekly.

I was comfortable in my neighborhood of other Catholic families transplanted into the small Dutch community where we lived.

I wasn't aware of the strong Reformed background in our town until I met Curt and his family. When I visited them for dinner the first time, his mom read from what I now know was an Our Daily Bread devotional. The more I heard her read over the months and years, the more interested I became in their brand of faith that was so full of meaning and depth. My interest grew as Curt's and my relationship did.

Since we were so in love, we decided to take the next logical step. After dating for five years, I finally became Mrs. Curt Boeve in November 1990. Despite my wanting children, we decided to wait to start a family. Three years later, Zachary Tyler was born on November 20, 1993. My first baby was here! My dream had come true.

The birth wasn't as easy as I had hoped, but after two and a half hours of pushing and many failed attempts at the "vacuum," he arrived—the first grandchild on both sides of our family. A few hours after the birth, as we reveled in the joy of new parenthood, my nurse—also my neighbor growing up—stopped in to visit. After talking to me for several minutes, she asked if she could hold Zachary. She mentioned he looked a little cold and maybe should visit the nursery to get warm. She took him out.

But he wasn't just cold; my newborn son had a pneumothorax, a hole in his lung that was causing it to collapse. They transferred my baby to a large hospital in nearby Grand Rapids that could care for him in the neonatal intensive care unit (NICU). He also had some bleeding on the brain and sleep apnea, all from the traumatic birth.

For the first time, I fell to my knees and prayed to the God I'd always felt was there. I prayed with a purpose, asking that all of Zach's problems go away. Almost as a challenge I ended my prayer with, "Are you for real, or will I be disappointed? I'm told you're the one I'm supposed to turn to when things are out of my control, so here I am."

I hadn't become a Christian at this point in my life. I didn't fully understand that God was bigger than the rituals I had grown up with, that he was more personal than the Jesus I saw suffering on the cross at my childhood church. But I realized afterward that there is power in prayer, which I had seen in Curt's family all along. After Zachary came home twelve days later a completely healthy baby, I began to understand this faith a little more. God is personal, and does answer prayer. I found myself feeling like I needed to get on my knees to pray, but I didn't have a purpose or enough understanding yet.

There wasn't a lot in my life that made me think I needed to have a deeper faith. Life was as perfect as I thought it could be. When you're young and have what you dreamed about all your life, there is a comfortableness in that.

Yet I continued to learn more about this Jesus in the years that followed and as the babies kept coming. Jordan

Lee was born on February 26, 1996, and Spencer James on June 20, 1998. I couldn't believe that I had three little boys ages four and under. I never pictured myself as an all-boy mom, but was pleasantly surprised to see how each one of them was so different. I loved dressing them alike so they would be adorable in pictures, which they were at the time. Though later, those pictures brought us some good laughs and great memories.

Those years were good ones. We were a family of five, with a great husband and three fantastic boys. We were building a new house as I drove the "mom minivan." Life couldn't get much better than that, could it?

My faith hadn't grown much in those years despite us attending Curt's church faithfully. I gained head knowledge, perhaps, but not heart knowledge from all those Bible studies I participated in. I just didn't have the knowledge base that so many of my friends at the church did. They'd grown up with the Bible stories told so often and songs sung weekly in Sunday school. That lack of knowledge seemed like one part of why my faith wasn't progressing.

Curt's parents attended that Reformed church as well, and they were delighted to see their grandsons running around the building each week. The closeness of family really appealed to me, with so much family within a ten to fifteen minute drive. We moved along through life with little disruption, a happy family leading a happy life.

As perfect as our lives seemed, however, something was amiss. I felt it when I was pregnant with Spencer. Something was happening with Curt; he was acting strangely but I couldn't put my finger on what was going on. Once our third son arrived, life was crazy. I didn't pay much attention to the subtle messages I had sensed.

Give careful thought to the paths for your feet and be steadfast in all your ways. —Proverbs 4:26

Reflection Questions

1. What events in your life have brought you closer to God?

2. What specifically did you learn about God through these events?

3. What is the timeline of your faith journey?

4. How have you dealt with unexpected circumstances in your life?

5. Who were the spiritual mentors who played a role in your life?

Hope Reflection

Faith is something to be used at any time and in any situation. Our faith journeys are unique paths designed by God and are processes unique to each of us. We can't speed them up or make them different than they are. Each journey is about walking the steps God had laid out and about facing, with his strength, the events that happen in our lives.

Prayer, reading the Bible, and attending church are all essential parts of the journey and help us develop the faith we need, as well as the hope that strengthens us, as we walk the paths of our lives.

Journal

_____

_____

_____

_____

_____

_____

_____

_____

_____

_____

_____

_____

_____

_____

_____

_____

_____

_____

_____

_____

_____

Prayer

Dear God, thank you for being a good Father I can trust. I might not always understand your ways, but I know you love me and are working all things out for my good. Your faithfulness on my journey reminds me that I can depend on you now, and I am confident in the hope you give me for my future. In Jesus' name, Amen.

CHAPTER THREE

A Family Destroyed

"Let your hopes, not your hurts, shape your future."

—ROBERT H. SCHULLER

I went back to work when Spencer was six weeks old. I cut hair two nights a week at a local salon, which allowed me to be home with the boys during the day plus get some adult time talking to clients. The boys could have daddy time on those nights. It was an ideal situation that didn't require childcare juggling and expenses.

On my second night back to work, I got home a little early. One of the boys was crying downstairs, but I knew Curt was with him so decided to pick up toys and blankets scattered around the living room. When I picked up one of the blankets, a folded piece of paper fell out. I picked it up, wondering how folded paper got in a child's blanket.

I read it. My heart felt like it was pounding outside my chest. The note was addressed to my husband from one of his female coworkers. She wrote about how in love she was with him and how she couldn't wait to spend the rest of their lives together. There was more, of course. I felt like the breath had been taken right out of my body. Talk about being in shock.

Yet during the last couple of months of my pregnancy, I had started to question some things that weren't adding up. Things like time away without explanation. Money spent on mysterious things. When I asked Curt about it, he told me I was paranoid and that my not trusting him made him want to do whatever I was thinking he was doing. I accepted his answers and his condemnation, and tried to move on despite my gut telling me something was off. Now I knew I wasn't crazy because I had proof. My worst nightmare was true.

I confronted him that night and our lives began spinning out of control. I had so many up-and-down moments because of what I'd discovered, but also because of the hormones raging in my postpartum body. I asked myself all kinds of questions: "How does something so 'perfect' end up like this?" "Was I married to someone I never really knew?" "Why was I still in love and he wasn't?" Questions rolled through my mind like an out-of-control roller coaster, not helped one bit by my roller-coaster hormones.

Almost immediately Curt told me he no longer loved me, that he was in love with the other woman, and that I was confusing him with all of my questions. Me confusing him? After several weeks of this crazy back-and-forth, I decided that I couldn't be married to a man who cheated on me and who was in love with someone else. I had packed clothes and other belongings for me and my three little boys and we were on the way to my parents' home. Suddenly Curt changed his mind and wanted to make our marriage work. I couldn't keep up with his sudden change of heart.

We were in the midst of a heated discussion about my leaving with the boys when his mom walked in.

"What's happening?" she asked.

"Please share your news, Curt. I'm sure your mom would love to hear what's going on," I said.

He told her I was leaving with the boys, and that he was in love with someone else. Her immediate response was shock, quickly followed by urging us to make our marriage work for our boys. And to keep everything quiet because it will be harder to move on if people are constantly questioning us about our marriage.

At that moment I decided to stay because I loved Curt's mom and respected her knowledge and wisdom. I figured she knew what she was talking about. I also kept everything quiet based on her advice. But our marriage was never the same again. I wanted Curt kissing my feet, begging for forgiveness, telling me how much he loved me and apologizing for what he had done to me and our sons. None of that ever happened. My trust level was at zero, which is an issue I struggled with even when our marriage was healthy. Curt's parents never argued, never disagreed, so it wasn't a surprise that they didn't want us to disagree, and if we did, it certainly couldn't be public. I asked Curt what was wrong with me: Was I ugly? Was I not doing enough? His answers never satisfied and he usually blamed me. If Curt had been sorry for what he'd done, wouldn't he be making changes in his life? He didn't, but we were still together, right?

I couldn't get past what happened, so I did the next best thing. I pretended his affair had never happened and swept it all under the rug. That didn't work too well either. The distrust and anger were eating me up on the inside, poisoning my soul and what was left of our relationship.

Several years into this détente, I had a brilliant idea. Let's have another baby, I suggested. I felt like I had missed out on Spencer's infant and toddler years because of the events in our marriage. Maybe a baby would make everything okay.

Emma Kathryn was born on August 15, 2002. Finally, a girl! I thought that God was *rewarding* me for staying in the marriage. Holding this baby girl was worth all the pain and suffering, all the dying inside. This time I would make every moment count, and how could God allow otherwise? Our perfect family was still intact and redeemed by a new baby daughter.

"Is this real?" I asked myself every time I saw my sweet Emma laying there in a pink and frilly outfit. Having a girl was so hard to believe after having three boys. I loved and cherished every moment with my little girl.

Emma was almost six months old when I started getting those same "feelings" I'd had before. I started seeing the same signs in Curt, but this time I wasn't going to let it control me. I confronted him, but he denied anything was going on. Then, on Valentine's Day in 2003, almost six months to the day after Emma's birth, I asked him again if everything was okay.

He turned and said, "I don't love you. I want to be done." There was no one else, he said, but he couldn't pretend anymore. I was just about at that place myself, but I had denied my thoughts by reminding myself I had a six-month-old, and boys ages four, six, and nine. What was I going to do?

What I did was put on waders and walk into the turbulent waters of saving our marriage. This time we sought out professional help, first at our large Christian Reformed church (we'd changed churches) and then through professional marriage counselors. We started to uncover the past as we lived apart. Curt left our home that February and was trying to figure out what he wanted. I was also starting to figure that out for myself. I was a wife, a mother, and a person who loved life, but there was so much more than that. Who was I?

Couples counseling was amazing in that I learned what a healthy marriage relationship looked like. I thought I had a healthy marriage all those years, but it turns out I did not. I soaked up every piece of information

I could and began reading Christian books and applying the concepts to my life as best I could. This was my new beginning, forged from the ashes of my marriage. I joined a neighbor's Bible study group and began learning who God really is. I learned to think of him as my earthly Father, not just a heavenly Father. He wasn't there just in troubled times (like Zach's difficult birth and hospitalization), but was in my life as if he was sitting on the couch across from me and carrying on a conversation. He hurt because I hurt. He cried when I cried. I wanted to know more about this God who was bringing back joy to my life despite the difficult circumstances. I was literally on fire for the Lord.

I didn't make any moves to end our marriage during 2003 because I thought it could survive. God had put us together, after all. I held onto the hope that God can make all things right and that with him, all things are possible. But there had been someone else in Curt's life all along, just as I suspected. A marriage takes two people, and I was the only one at that moment. The only person I told was our neighbor, a good friend of mine.

No one knew we were living apart during all those months, though he was at our home several times a week picking up the kids or coordinating rides to and from the many events we were involved in. People asked how we were doing, of course, because they saw him with another woman, but I never told them the truth. I eventually confided in a couple of girlfriends after one had seen him with that same woman.

I often fell to my knees at my bedroom window and cried out to God. He was the Savior of my life. God met me there multiple times a day and gave me the encouragement and courage that I needed. I would hold my Bible in my hands, crying out and asking for help because I couldn't go on. I would open the Bible and find a Scripture verse almost popping out from the page. So many refreshing words seemed meant just for me at the moments I needed them most. God was filling me with himself. I wasn't trying to fill myself with me or Curt or anyone else.

Finally, on Christmas Day 2003, ten months after Curt left our home, I received confirmation from God that I had given all I could give to my marriage and now had permission to move on. I had done all I could; so much weight was lifted from my shoulders. I felt freer than I had in years, free to live again. I felt as if God had plans for me and was preparing me for something new.

For sin, seizing the opportunity afforded by the commandment, deceived me, and through the commandment put me to death. So then, the law is holy, and the commandment is holy, righteous and good. —Romans 7:11–12

Reflection Questions

1. How has hiding or burying something—events, feelings, etc.—affected your life in negative ways?

2. How has prayer been part of your life during stressful events? If not, why not?

3. In what ways do you need to work on your marriage? Why now? Why not now?

4. When have you felt betrayed? How did you handle it?

5. How has God led you to move on from a difficult situation? How did it feel?

Hope Reflection

God calls us to be free, but not free to commit sins. Hiding or burying sin by distracting yourself or minimizing it only delays the process of rooting that sin out of your life. Doing so can also endanger yourself and others.

The gospel promises us eternal acceptance because of what Jesus did, not eternal rejection because of what we've done. God's grace gives us the assurance and confidence that we never again have to try to bury our sin. Those sins were dealt with, once and for all, when Jesus died on the cross.

Journal

_____

_____

_____

_____

_____

_____

_____

_____

_____

_____

_____

_____

_____

_____

_____

_____

_____

_____

_____

_____

_____

_____

_____

Prayer

Heavenly Father, I am so glad your arm is not too short to save me, to pull me out of difficult places in life. Forgive me for ignoring the Holy Spirit's warnings as I've jumped into treacherous waters that should have been avoided. Give me strength to walk away when I feel that nudge in my spirit that says, "Don't go there." I love you, Lord. Thank you for being my rescuer. In Jesus' name, Amen.

CHAPTER FOUR

A Life Renewed

"What gives me the most hope every day is God's grace; knowing that his grace is going to give me the strength for whatever I face, knowing that nothing is a surprise to God."

—RICK WARREN

I started 2004 in a good place. I knew our marriage was finally over—Curt filed for divorce early 2004—but I was looking forward, not backward. I'm not saying life was easy as a single mom, nor was my head in the clouds. It was difficult juggling daily activities on my own; I had to pick up more hours at the salon to make ends meet. I was responsible for everything, but I had a positive, God-centered outlook on life and looked forward to the path I was going to follow.

For almost a full year before our divorce was final, I had full custody of our four children. He saw them one night a week and every other weekend. Zach was only nine and Emma was an infant, so when our arrangement was presented to the court, the judge agreed. I asked Curt to explain to the boys what was going on, how he wouldn't be living with us anymore, and that mommy and daddy weren't going to be married anymore. The boys cried because they didn't understand what all this meant for them, but seemed to go on with their lives at church and at school. Zach, being the oldest, seemed to feel like he needed to play the role of father figure for his siblings and me. I had to say to him a couple of times that he didn't have to play the role of the father. It was not his job. He was a kid, after all, and we were the adults. I didn't want him to carry our issues on his back and grow up too soon.

On a Saturday night in January 2004, my girlfriend Kelly called and asked if I would like to come to her house for some girl time. Her husband was out and Curt had the kids, so I agreed that a little girl time wouldn't be amiss. In fact, a night with a friend sounded great!

We had a good time for a couple of hours before I said I needed to be leaving soon. It was getting late and I was tired. She asked me to stay for a bit longer so I could say hi to her husband who would be home soon. He walked in a bit later with his friend Dave in tow. Looking at my friend and her husband trying not to laugh, I realized this had been the scheme all along. Dave was also divorced, and these two thought we should meet each other.

Well, we talked for a couple of hours that night. It was so nice to relate to someone on so many different levels. I had told myself that I was never going to date again, much less marry. I had married a man I'd known since we were kids and that didn't turn out so well. Why would I want to start a new relationship so soon and risk being hurt again?

We had a great time that night, talking and laughing with our friends and each other. As I finally walked outside to leave, Dave accompanied me. He asked if he could have my cell phone number.

"Why?" I asked.

"It was so refreshing to talk to someone who knows exactly how I'm feeling and what I've been going through," he said.

We exchanged numbers and I turned to leave.

"Can I give you a hug?" he asked.

We hugged and he leaned in for a kiss.

"I can't do this," I said. "I'm really sorry, but I'm not ready for that yet."

He apologized and we turned and left.

I was driving home when my phone rang. Yes, it was Dave calling to apologize again for how he had acted. He told me he is usually a gentleman and how sorry he was to have put me in the position of having to say no to him. I accepted his apology, of course, and we agreed to talk soon. Now that was a gentleman, I said to myself, a gentleman calling to make things right. He was genuine, I thought.

I thought a lot about the things Dave and I had talked about. I knew I wanted to get excited about meeting such a nice guy, but quickly put up my invisible wall to protect myself from getting hurt. I knew I didn't want to feel that kind of hurt again.

But when he called the next night at nine thirty, I picked up the phone and we talked and talked. After three hours on the phone, we agreed that phone conversations—this was before texting—were a great way to get to know each other. About a month later, he asked if I would cut his hair, which I agreed to do. I thought this would be a safe way to get to know him in person because we hadn't seen each other since that night we met. We decided that he would bring his three kids over to meet my four kids while I cut his hair, sort of a trial run to see if our kids would get along. They got along great! They were laughing and giggling like they had known each other forever.

Dave and his ex-wife had been divorced more than a year by this time and shared custody of their three children. His daughters, Alexandra and Brandi were twelve and ten, and his son Collin was almost seven. Brandi and my Zach were five weeks apart in age, and my son Jordan and Alex shared the same birthday though four years apart. Collin fit right in between my boys. The older girls doted on baby Emma, who was about eighteen months old.

Over the next couple of months, my walls started to break down as we got to know each other. Dave was taking his three kids and two of their friends to Gulf Shores, Alabama, for Spring Break, always a big event here in Michigan. He came to see me the night before they left, leaning in to give me a hug before he walked out the door, praying as he usually did when we parted. This time he softly touched my cheeks, looked me in the eyes and said, "I have something to tell you."

"What?" I asked, fearing the worst.

"I love you."

I just stared at him and started to cry.

"I really appreciate you saying that, but I can't say the words back to you because I'm too afraid to get hurt again," I got out between the tears.

"I wasn't expecting you to say it back and that's okay," he said. "I will wait for you."

I couldn't believe what just happened. There were good guys in the world after all, and God had put this one, David Tidd, in my life because we needed each other.

I took time while he was gone to examine my heart, reflect, pray, and think about what life could look like with him and his kids. Was I in a good enough place to take the next step? Were my children? God had given me clear indications during this time that Dave was the kind of man I needed and wanted. I wasn't pushing my own agenda but was relying on God to lead the way. And he did.

When Dave returned, I was thrilled to see him. I had truly missed him, and in his absence came to know that I was ready to take the next step. When we saw each other, I ran up and hugged him and showered him with kisses. He seemed surprised at my openness, then he handed me a small pile of letters. He had taken the time each day he was gone to write me a letter. Each one included Scripture and reasons why he felt God put us together. These letters were amazing, revealing again to me that God meant for us to be together.

We loved each other, both of us now walking the same path. We saw each other several times a week and on weekends for the next nine months, growing closer as we dated and got to know each other even better and our children got to know one another better as well. That fall, before we were engaged, I got a call from the missionary parents of a neighbor.

"We're coming back to the area next spring and need a place to live. We heard you might be selling your house," she said.

I was surprised, but I also knew I would be selling in the spring per Curt's and my divorce agreement. My plan was to get Zach through fifth grade, then sell and split the profits with Curt. In God's great plan, and through this missionary, I didn't have to put the house on the market or worry even one minute about selling it. Dave and I knew we would get engaged, but we weren't sure when because so much depended on selling the house. This was one more point of clarification for me.

A year after we first met, Dave asked me to marry him. Before he did so, he'd asked my parents and my oldest son for their permission to marry me. Zachary's response was, "Of course! I love seeing my mom laugh again. You make her so happy."

We got married on July 30, 2005, with all seven of our children, ranging in age from almost three to thirteen, in the wedding. One of my favorite things about the wedding was when each child poured a different color sand into a clear vase. It signified to all of us how a natural "blending" takes place and how beautiful that blending is.

That blending truly was beautiful as we created a new family. Our kids loved being together and they cared for one another. Dave and I accepted each other's kids as if they were our own, and we as a new family shared something that only God could have arranged.

I look back even now and see how beautifully orchestrated our new lives were. Why? Because it wasn't my plan and I wasn't in charge. God had planted those seeds years ago as I sought to obey him and put my hope in him. As I obeyed, new life began. Our new lives were wonderful and full of hope, with a great husband, great kids, and a bright future.

Place me like a seal over your heart,
like a seal on your arm;
for love is as strong as death,
its jealousy unyielding as the grave.
It burns like blazing fire,
like a mighty flame.
Many waters cannot quench love;
rivers cannot sweep it away.
If one were to give
all the wealth of one's house for love,
it would be utterly scorned.

—Song of Songs 8:6–7

Reflection Questions

1. How have you withdrawn into shame or anger over the events in your life?

2. How did that withdrawal affect your life in negative ways?

3. What part does fear play in your life? What are your biggest fears?

4. How has God directed your path out of shame, fear, or anger?

5. How have you seen God making something good from something awful?

Hope Reflection

I like the verses from Song of Songs because they talk about love being as strong as death. I never imagined that I would understand what the writer said so completely. I was so fearful based on what I thought love was. My life was bound by fear and anxiety, so afraid of losing someone I loved that I was almost paralyzed.

Then I lost two people I loved deeply. I never would have believed that I could love again, but God showed me that he promised me a life full of faith, truth, hope, peace, joy, and—the greatest of all—love. Love is a priceless gift that cannot be bought. We can only accept love from our spouse, family, children, and friends as God's gift, given because he loves us!

Journal

_____

_____

_____

_____

_____

_____

_____

_____

_____

_____

_____

_____

_____

_____

_____

_____

_____

_____

_____

_____

_____

Prayer

Father God, thank you that you are a God who stands with me right where I am. Thank you for helping me focus on the present, for reminding me that you call me to keep my eyes focused on you and to trust the plans you have for me.

Forgive me, Lord, for looking back at a life you've helped me leave behind. I trust you, Jesus, and I believe in your perfect plan for me. Please help me remember to turn all my anxieties and fears over to you, to lean into your Word and promises. In Jesus' name, Amen.

CHAPTER FIVE

Gifts for a Lifetime

"The work goes on, the cause endures, the hope still lives and the dreams shall never die."

—EDWARD KENNEDY

Zach, Emma, and I were driving one gloomy day, as many days are during the Michigan winter, when the sun peaked briefly through the clouds. My four-year-old piped up from the back seat, "Isn't that pretty?"

"Yes, it is very pretty, Emma," I responded.

Her brother said nothing, so as any four-year-old little sister would do, she kept repeating the question over and over until he finally answered.

"Emma! I can see the sun. Wow. Thanks for telling me how pretty it is, because I couldn't see it!" Zach said.

We both laughed when she responded with, "Be nice, Zachy!"

The sun soon disappeared behind a cloud and all was quiet in the back seat until, "Mommy, how do you *goed* to heaven?"

I was taken aback, asking her to repeat what she said. "I said, how do you *goed* to heaven?"

I asked myself how I was going to answer such a question as Zach and I looked at each other with blank faces. Emma continued to stare at the cloudy-then-sunny sky. I heard Zach say, "Good luck, Mom." I took a few seconds to gather my thoughts.

"Well, when people die, they go up to heaven. God takes their soul but their earthly body is left here," I said.

I turned to look at her and found her staring at me. I could see that her mind was working hard, so I waited for more questions. I told her that when she got older she would understand better and she was good with that.

My sweet Emma's question about heaven occurred a couple of weeks before the accident. It was one of many blessings that I carry with me today and that I held close after my children were taken from me. There were several of these blessings that I can't call coincidences. I see them as glimpses of God's work in me and for me that bring him glory.

Sometimes glimpses of my little girl would almost take my breath away. I feel like those glimpses were preparing me for her loss. Sometimes I felt that hitch in my breath when she walked around a corner when I wasn't expecting her or when she suddenly spoke after being quiet for a while. It was a strange feeling and one that I didn't pay much attention to except to realize again how much I loved my daughter.

We had a routine when all the kids went to bed. Emma was last, of course, as she had to see everyone before it was her turn. We started in Collin and Spencer's room with all of us saying prayers there. She would crawl into the beds and give each boy a hug and kiss. We then headed to Jordan and Zach's room, where she waited for them to get under the covers. Each one got a hug and a kiss. Occasionally, though, Zach would have what she called "zips" that she felt she needed to pop. Most of the time this didn't go well, but she was feisty and would win the battle in the end.

Her stepsisters Alex and Brandi were next in line, and after them it was her turn for bed. She would try just about anything to stall, and once in a while, we got sidetracked. A week or so before the accident, she decided to stall by measuring everyone's feet and hands against her own.

She was clever; soon we were all measuring each other's hands and feet. We talked about whose hands had gotten bigger, whether toes were curled or straight, short or long.

We had a lot of laughs that night though it took some time to get Emma to bed. But what a gift for me to remember after the awful events that were to come. Even then, God was looking out for me. The doctors and nurses at the hospital created imprints of Emma's hands and feet and gave them to Dave as we left. The box was tied with a pink ribbon, but I didn't open it for several months until I found it in a closet. I don't remember receiving the box, nor knew what was in it. How could they have known what those little hands and feet would mean to me later? They couldn't know, but what they did was surely part of God's plan to provide me with solace and peace.

I have always been a city girl, or as big-city as Holland, Michigan, can be, but Dave lived in the country. We built a home there together, where we still live. Now it's the most beautiful and peaceful place on Earth but I didn't always think so, mostly because traveling to stores required thought and preparation. The twenty-minute drive meant that I couldn't quickly return to the store if I forgot something. I was used to everything I needed being less than five minutes away.

Dave, the country guy that he is, had his kids showing steers and pigs through 4-H for years. After we married, my sons Zach and Jordan joined right in. The smells, work, and amount of time it required took me some time to adjust to, but I loved seeing my kids have so much fun. Watching my husband in his element made me love him even more. Zachary took such a liking to the animals and the farm show atmosphere that I think he was finding his niche in life. Raising and showing animals was a huge part of Alexandra's life, and to have Zach join her grew the bond between new brother and sister exponentially.

On Saturday, January 13, Dave, myself, my mom Becky, and Zach hopped into the truck to go pick up a new 4-H steer for Alex. Zach was in the back seat behind Dave.

As we drove, I glanced to my left and did a double take. My breath was taken away as I looked at my son. I couldn't believe how old he looked. I stared, taking in the details of his size ten and a half feet resting on the floor mat like a grown man. He was five foot eight inches tall already and he was just thirteen. I continued to stare until he asked what I was looking at. I said it was nothing and turned to look out the truck's front window.

Another event I remember so clearly happened the next day. I was in the bathroom curling my hair as I got ready to go to church. Out of nowhere, there stood Emma in the doorway. She startled me so much that I let out a small scream. She looked like an angel standing there in her favorite long nightgown, hair disheveled from sleep. She was not a morning girl and didn't love to wake up quickly. I picked her up and sat with her for a few minutes. Something seemed off, but when I asked if she felt okay she said she did.

She was quiet before church and remained so at church. I was on the praise team that morning so I wasn't sitting with the family. When it came time for the children's sermon, Emma went right up to Pastor Marc DeWaard and sat on his lap. This was unusual because she normally stayed at the back of the group of children. When she returned to the pew, she asked Daddy Dave to pick her up. She wrapped her arms around his neck like she was holding on for dear life. I thought for sure she was getting sick. I can't say for sure, but I think she knew in some way that something was going to happen. She was doing what she could to understand.

When I think about it now, perhaps God gave me those special moments to just soak her and Zach in, to cement in my mind what each child looked like, sounded like, smelled like. There are so many things that stick in our minds forever, good and bad and for unknown reasons. But those times when Emma and Zach took my breath away are so precious now. I didn't have them for long—Emma only four years and five months—but I have those memories and mental pictures of them that I believe were intentional gifts from the God who knew what I would need in the years to come.

I live each day knowing that I will see my children again. I live with the hope of a future with them, and I remember each special moment with joy until that time.

> *Now this is eternal life: that they know you, the only true God, and Jesus Christ, whom you have sent. I have brought you glory on earth by finishing the work you gave me to do.* —John 17:3–4

Reflection Questions

1. Have you ever glimpsed someone you love and caught your breath? How did it make you feel?

2. When have you sensed that God has given you a glimpse of something special?

3. What memories of your loved ones do you treasure?

4. How have you recorded those memories? If you haven't, find a way to do so.

5. What do you believe the future holds for loved ones you have lost? Why?

Hope Reflection

It brings me pure joy to know that one day I will see my babies again. I think I scared my husband the day I told him I couldn't wait to get to heaven and was ready to go. I wasn't talking about ending my life, but about the beauty beyond all understanding that God promises.

I was given small glimpses of heaven thanks to my children. God gave me those glimpses before Zach and Emma left this earth when their work here was finished. When they did, my work began in a whole new way. I take on that work with pleasure. God has given me more than I could have imagined in this race for Jesus!

Journal

_____

_____

_____

_____

_____

_____

_____

_____

_____

_____

_____

_____

_____

_____

_____

_____

_____

_____

_____

_____

_____

_____

Prayer

Heavenly Father, I thank you every day for those "glimmers" you blessed me with. Help others who have lost loved ones be able to recognize those gifts they were given as well. Each one is a sign of the life we are promised from you, when our race is finished here. In Jesus' name, Amen.

CHAPTER SIX

Living in Hope

"*The very least you can do in your life is figure out what you hope for. And the most you can do is live inside that hope. Not admire from a distance, but live right in it under its roof.*"

—BARBARA KINGSOLVER

*H*ope is the word I cling to, what I call my *life word*. Hope keeps me positive in a world in which it's easy to be the opposite: hope-less. We have that broader hope as Christ followers, knowing one day we'll be with Jesus in heaven. We can live each day in the hope of Jesus, whether our days are easy or difficult.

I have always been and will likely always be that person who needs to be in control. It's a daily battle for me as Satan tries to make me believe that Jesus doesn't care and that I need to run my world. Remember when I tried to make a deal with God when Zachary was in the hospital after his birth? That was me trying to gain the upper hand. I knew that I did not, based on the fact that Zach was sick and hospitalized. God was ultimately in control, as well as the doctors for Zach's care, but I was trying to see how big God was by having him prove it to me by healing Zach.

I prayed so many prayers, ending each one with an ultimatum. If Zach would heal and be healthy, I would rely more on God. God indeed chose to heal Zach, answering my mother's prayer. That seed, sprinkled by Zach's healing, began to take root in me regardless of my questionable motives in giving God an ultimatum. Despite myself, God's love found a home.

> *"Therefore, with minds that are alert and fully sober, set your hope on the grace to be brought to you when Jesus Christ is revealed at his coming. As obedient children, do not conform to the evil desires you had when you lived in ignorance. But just as he who called you is holy, so be holy in all you do, for it is written: Be holy, because I am holy."*
> —1 Peter 1:13–16

After Zach came home, I did just as I promised. We started going to Sunday school at the church Curt and I attended. To be honest, I felt pretty low on the ladder of faith. How, after attending church as a child and as a young adult, did I not know all this stuff? These people knew so much about God and the Bible. It would have been easy to walk away because I felt so inadequate, but I didn't. I had promised God, after all, and if I didn't keep that promise

I thought maybe I'd get struck by lightning or, worse, my son would be taken from me for real this time.

"There the angel of the Lord appeared to him in flames of fire from within a bush. Moses saw that though the bush was on fire it did not burn up."
—Exodus 3:2

God spoke to Moses through a burning bush, which was quite an unexpected prop for God to use. Yet Moses was willing to follow God and trust what he would do. God had some surprises in store for this man who had fled his home forty years before, but Moses trusted him. I'd say that God has the same thing in store for us—surprises and plans we know nothing about—if we're willing to acknowledge his signs and follow him.

Looking back, I now know that I did not put God into the equation of Curt's and my marriage, much less our individual lives. Going through the affairs and later a divorce, all with four young children, was not what I expected my life to be and I wouldn't wish it on anyone. Yet, in the years following and through counseling, I asked God to reveal himself and to show me what he wanted me to learn from those times. One thing I learned is that God wasn't our base, we didn't turn to him or let him be in control. We wanted to control our own lives, which clearly didn't work so well.

Then I met David. God showed me through him what a healthy marriage looked like with God at the center. As I learned and grew, hope was revived once again. God met me at every step of our courtship and marriage, with Dave leading the way. When we first met that night at our friends' house, I shared that my faith was a large part of my life and had helped me have peace despite the horrible events of the last years.

That trust in God, and the trust I still have, is still a work in progress. Satan knows where he can hit me and how to bring me to my knees (remember that issue I have with control?), catching me off guard. Dave gets it because he has his own struggles; sometimes he has to step back and let me work through my stuff. He knew I came with baggage, but he also knew I came with hope. My hope is in Jesus Christ and that is the truth. It's also true that I sometimes fail and put my hope in my husband, but I know in my heart of hearts that Jesus truly is the answer.

> *"For I know the plans I have for you," declares the Lord, "plans to prosper you and not to harm you, plans to give you* hope *and a future" (roman added).* —Jeremiah 29:11

One of the first gifts Dave gave me was a picture frame with this verse on it. It soon became our family's life verse. We know that God knows our future and promises boundless hope. This doesn't mean we'll be spared pain, suffering, or hardship, but it does mean God will see us through that pain and offers us a glorious ending in heaven.

You're probably asking yourself right now how any mother can come away from losing two of her children and still glorify God. Time. It used to make me mad when I heard people say, "Time heals." I would think, "Oh really? Do you just forget what happened over time? Your pain just stops?" Or better yet, "Do you know what it feels like to lose a piece of yourself?"

Now, thirteen years later, the pain isn't as sharp as it once was. It's always there and will never go away, but it's no longer at the forefront of my mind every minute of the day. I wake up every single morning missing Zach and Emma, but I choose every single day not to let that ache take me down to the depths.

It wasn't always this way. The first couple of years after the accident, I ran in "mom survival mode." I took Spencer and Jordan to therapy and doctor appointments and any other medical things they needed. We left the rehabilitation hospital after a couple of weeks and started running through life. There was no time for me because I had to be strong for my boys. Any quiet time I had was spent sitting in waiting rooms. If I sat down at home, I felt as if I couldn't relax and just be happy in the moment.

My boys had lost a lot as well: their dad, brother, and sister. How could any of us find happiness again? I didn't have the joy for life I had once felt, which is no surprise. My home brought up memories of the past, the children I would never see again this side of heaven. I saw Zach and Emma's lockers when we walked in the house every day, their stuff untouched. Their rooms were exactly how they had left them. Somehow, I had to walk past and not curl up into a ball on their beds and feel sorry for myself. I couldn't do that; I couldn't add more pain to what my boys already carried.

I wondered if this is how life would be from now on. I was starting to lose my will to live. I didn't want to talk to anyone; mostly I just wanted to feel sorry for myself. Yet I chose daily to put one foot in front of the other for my family. I did it because I had to.

I hit rock bottom two years after the accident. Yes, it took a long time. Dave happened to be at home that morning, which could only have been God's grace. I couldn't take another step, couldn't continue on. I needed help and I needed it NOW! I was sobbing like I hadn't sobbed in a long time, with Dave holding me. I told him how I felt like I was in a deep pit, trying with all I had to climb out, but my nails only scraped the dirt and I couldn't move. This was the kind of grief I had read about, but never pictured myself experiencing. The hope I had always carried with me was gone, and it was gone because I was angry at God. Why did he do this? How could he have let this happen? What did he want from me?

He hadn't answered any of those questions for two long years. In my eyes, God was unfair. Why had he given me these precious children, one whose life he had saved as a newborn, just to take them away from me?

I began going to a counselor that a friend recommended in January 2009. I knew immediately that she was the right fit, that God had hand picked her for me. She was the light shining into that pit I couldn't escape, the light that reminded me about the God we serve. (In fact, she is the one who first said that one day I would write a book.) I slowly began to return to my knees at my bedroom window, to once again be filled with the hope that I so desperately needed. I cried and cried, apologizing to God for demanding answers according to my timing, questioning his goodness, questioning his plan for my life.

God cried too, saying to me, "I'm not upset with you, daughter. I've been patiently waiting for you. I hurt because you hurt, I cried when you cried, and I knew you would come back. Reset your eyes back on that hope, and hold on for the ride I've got in store for you."

My confession and falling to my knees, literally and figuratively, revealed the submission of my heart and the fallow ground ready to be planted. God could once again do his work in and through me. I was ready.

"Shadrach, Meshach and Abednego replied to him, 'King Nebuchadnezzar, we do not need to

defend ourselves before you in this manner. If we are thrown into the blazing furnace, the God we serve is able to deliver us from it, and he will deliver us from Your Majesty's hand. But even if he does not, we want you to know, O king, that we will not serve your gods or worship the image of gold you have set up.'" —Daniel 3:16–18

These three young men were determined to be faithful in Babylon because they trusted God regardless of their circumstances. If God allowed everything in our lives to be perfect all the time, we wouldn't need faith. We choose to be faithful whether God intervenes on our behalf or not. Our eternal reward will be worth the suffering we endure.

This was a hard concept for me to swallow, as I'm sure it is for anyone who has lost loved ones. But each of us can choose to trust God, see his hand, and recognize the hope that eternity promises.

Not only so, but we ourselves, who have the firstfruits of the Spirit, groan inwardly as we wait eagerly for our adoption to sonship, the redemption of our bodies. For in this hope we were saved. But hope that is seen is no hope at all. Who hopes for what they already have? But if we hope for what we do not yet have, we wait for it patiently. —Romans 8:23–25

Reflection Questions

1. Where do you see yourself needing to be in control? How does this work for you?

2. When have you given ultimatums to God? Why?

3. How have you muscled through tough times because you felt you had to? What caused you to stop muscling through?

4. When have you felt God has been unfair? Why?

5. How have you lived in the hope God offers? How have you seen that hope change your life?

Hope Reflection

Every day I have to decide whether God is going to be in control of my life, or I am. The choice isn't easy. The more life feels out of control—divorce, tragedy, death, spouse, kids, job—the harder we try to control it. We want to stop that spinning-out-of-control feeling because so much doesn't make sense. It's easy to just give up.

But giving up or taking control aren't good options. The only option is to surrender to God. The moment I choose to surrender is the moment I fall to my knees and put my hands in the air. There is no more freeing feeling than allowing God to take the weight from off my tired shoulders.

Journal

_____

_____

_____

_____

_____

_____

_____

_____

_____

_____

_____

_____

_____

_____

_____

_____

_____

_____

_____

_____

_____

_____

_____

Prayer

Lord, I want to surrender myself to you. It is scary to feel out of control, especially when it feels like my life is falling apart. This broken world we live in wants us to believe that we are in total control of our destiny.

I come to you confessing my need for you in my life. I pray that your grace and mercy will lead and guide me, that you would take control. Help me, Lord, to give that control of my life to you in every way and to become the person you would have me to be. In Jesus' name, Amen.

CHAPTER SEVEN

A Thankful Heart

"When I was young, my ambition was to be one of the people who made a difference in this world. My hope is to leave the world a little better for having been there."

—JIM HENSON

I didn't think I'd like living in a small town. Holland, Michigan, isn't that big, but it was big enough to have all the stores I needed close at hand plus good schools, coffee shops, restaurants, and cute boutiques. But Hamilton? Out in the middle of nowhere, twenty minutes from the stores I frequented?

Yet God knew that a small, close-knit community was just what we needed. Dave and his kids had long been part of Hamilton life, but I and my children had only lived there a year and a half before the tragedy. God had put us exactly where he wanted us and we needed to be there for the next chapters of our lives.

The support we received and our friends' and neighbors' downpour of love was more than we could have dreamed when they found out Zach and Emma had been killed in the car accident. Often a tragedy like this brings a community together, but our little town went above and beyond. Everyone has my unending gratitude.

We received so much love from friends and family while Jordan and Spencer remained in the hospital and later in the rehabilitation hospital. And it didn't let up even after they were able to come home. Folks took days off work to sit with one of the boys while we made funeral arrangements. Family members spent the night at the hospital so Dave and I could get "good sleep." That was a sacrifice on their parts because nobody sleeps in a hospital. A dear friend picked up Jordan at the hospital so he could come to the visitation early to join the family.

My friends from high school spent late nights putting together picture boards for Zach and Emma's funeral and visitations, something I couldn't have done myself. They organized things at our home, including doing laundry and storing the huge amounts of food that people brought over. We had to begin turning it away because we didn't have any more room to store it!

The care and support extended well beyond our small town. Somehow it got out that Jordan loved Michigan State University and Spencer loved the University of Michigan. They each got a care package from the coach of their beloved teams wishing them a speedy recovery. Even the Detroit Lions sent a care package! These gestures were wonderful and helped, I believe, to take their minds off the physical and emotional pain of their loss and injuries.

The Hamilton schools were wonderful as well. Teachers and administrators at all levels—we had kids from elementary to high school—allowed us the time we needed for our kids to try to pick up the pieces before returning to school. They understood that the children would need extra support, and they knew what that support looked like. Teachers knew the kids and were tuned in to their needs. This was a blessing to Dave and I as parents.

In 2015, Hamilton Community Schools completed an outdoor basketball court and named it the Zach Boeve Memorial Basketball Court, because he loved basketball so much. It is placed between the middle and high schools near the baseball field. The project was started in 2007, and revived by Jordan's girlfriend, Cameron Everse, who was a high school senior at the time.

Haven Reformed Church in Hamilton was a special blessing to us in this terrible time. Dave had grown up in that church, and they came alongside us immediately. They provided food for the family at the visitation, they held a prayer vigil the night of the accident, they brought meals, and provided us with gas cards because they knew we would be traveling often to Grand Rapids for medical appointments. Pastor Marc DeWaard protected us and acted and spoke on our behalf to the media and community. This was huge for us and a reminder of how in a small community people are eager to help.

Occasionally I pull out the large tote filled with cards and other well-wishes we received after the deaths of Zach and Emma. Looking at that physical outpouring of support touches me to this day and reminds me that God's love is shown through the hands of people. Just sending a card says so much. Fixing a meal, driving a child to school or sports practice, creating a memory board, just sitting next to a grieving mom is all part of how God used people in our lives.

I surely cannot list every person who expressed their concern, care, and love for us during that horrible time in our lives. But I know each of us felt the love then and still do to this day.

I wonder what we would have done without the outpouring of love after the accident. How would we have handled it all? What do people do who don't have that? It prompts me to think about how I can be God's hands and feet to people who are in crisis.

The most important thing I can do is pray, but a close second is to just be there. We so appreciated our friends and family coming alongside us as we mourned, faced extended hospital stays, and had other children to care for and help grieve. You may believe that saying nothing is better than saying the wrong thing at a time of tragedy. To be honest, sometimes it is. But most of the time, a simple

"We're praying for you" or "We love you" is enough. A simple card, a simple meal is enough.

Those going through tragedy often can't think straight, can't do simple things like dishes and laundry. That's where you can step in to help. Clean a counter. Fold a load of laundry. Mow a lawn. Rake leaves.

Also know, though, when to leave. Those who are grieving and in shock are in no shape to tend to your needs. They are in no shape to entertain you, prepare food for you, or answer endless questions. Simply offer your love and condolences, meet the needs you see, and allow them space and quiet.

Everyone grieves differently. Everyone handles tragedy differently. Being attuned to those differences—which may be very different from your needs but not wrong—will help you help others who mourn. Be God's heart by being his hands and feet.

Suggestions for helping those who are grieving:

1. Acknowledge their loss by remembering the loved one who has died. Tell stories about that person and let the grieving person know that you haven't forgotten his or her legacy.
2. When the loss is fresh and you enter their home, remember that the people left behind don't have the energy or thought processes to entertain you or start conversations. Keep your visit short and offer love, prayers, a meal. Don't linger.

3. As the grief process unfolds, ask how the person left behind is doing, offer a prayer or a hug. Don't ignore the person's pain and loss and make everything about you in an effort to avoid hard conversations.

4. If you have experienced deep grief, don't offer advice and a to-do list for another's grief process. Simply listen and say "I get it."

5. Don't be afraid or uneasy if your grieving friend cries easily and at "strange" things. Let her cry, give her a hug, and a little space.

A new command I give you: Love one another. As I have loved you, so you must love one another. By this everyone will know that you are my disciples, if you love one another. —John 13:34–35

Reflection Questions

1. What has helped you deal with tragedy—cards, simple words, actions?

2. What do you typically do when faced with others' tragedy? How does doing so make you feel?

3. How have you seen others goof up when it comes to helping others?

4. What are some concrete steps you can take to help others in a time of tragedy?

5. How can your church or community come alongside those who are grieving?

Hope Reflection

When tragedy strikes a small community, it is devastating. That tragedy can be a bridge to connect one another, or it can divide them because tragedy is something no one wants to have to face. People are faced with choosing to love the hurting with compassion, or avoiding them because they don't know what to do or say.

As we grow in our walk with the Lord, the more aware we become of the interests and needs of others. God leads us and helps us to help those in need, whether through a kind word, a hug, a meal, or something more substantial. Take a look at your prayer list and see whether the list is full of your own needs or those of others. God can and will use you to answer someone else's prayer.

Journal

_____

_____

_____

_____

_____

_____

_____

_____

_____

_____

_____

_____

_____

_____

_____

_____

_____

_____

_____

Prayer

Oh Father, please use me as you answer the prayers of others in need. Teach me to be generous in giving my time, my talents, and my resources. Help me be willing and available to follow you, however and wherever you lead. In Jesus' name, Amen.

CHAPTER EIGHT

God in the Choices

"I don't think of all the misery,
but of the beauty that still remains."

—ANNE FRANK

Spencer was eight years old when the accident occurred. He had a traumatic brain injury (TBI), as well as broke every bone on the left side of his face including the eye socket, his nose, and his jaw. Not one bone was broken anywhere else in his body. His little-boy head had taken the full force of the collision, which also included gashes from the glass cutting his face and a punctured eardrum.

His room in the ICU was a glass-walled room. From the hallway he looked just about normal because we saw only the right side of his face. But walking in, we could see the full extent of his injuries. His left side was black and blue, his head was swollen, and his left eye was just a slit. His head was wrapped in gauze. We could only watch and wait. Doctors couldn't fix the bones in his face yet because of his instability at that point. A TBI is often just a waiting game.

We received word on Wednesday, January 17, just two days after the accident, that ten-year-old Jordan would be released later that day. Insurance wouldn't let him stay in the hospital if he met every expectation to be released, which I understood, but how was I supposed to be at home with him, in the ICU with Spencer, and plan a funeral for the other two? I had the brilliant idea to call our pediatrician to see if there was anything he could do to help Jordan stay in the hospital.

After stammering around for a bit, he said, "I will do whatever it takes; you can count on it." Dave and I left to make funeral arrangements.

When we returned in the late afternoon, we found that Jordan had spiked a fever. By law the hospital couldn't send him home until they discovered the reason behind the fever. We so appreciated our pediatrician being willing to step in should he be needed, but we also knew that God had been at work. While a fever isn't good, it prevented my son having to be home without me. While the family was wonderfully willing to be there with him, I wanted to be the one to go home with him for the first time after the accident. The first time I went home after the accident was horrible; I didn't want the same thing for him.

As we stood outside Spencer's room that day talking with family, getting updates on what had been happening, I could see the nurse staring at Spencer, who had been in a coma since the accident. She looked concerned. She stood up as I walked in and said, "Spencer's been a little agitated the last fifteen minutes or so. I'm keeping an eye on him."

I walked up to the bed and touched Spencer's arm. As soon as I did, he moved. She jumped up again. We could see he was trying to talk! The nurse was calmly telling him that he couldn't talk because the tube down his throat would damage his vocal cords if he did. Spencer was having none of that. This child who had been in a deep coma, sat straight up in bed. He was trying to swing his legs over the side of the bed, telling us that he needed to go to the bathroom. His nurse remained calm, but was clearly panicking. He needed to stay in bed, remain calm, and not try to talk.

She was frantic but I was ecstatic. My son was awake—very agitated of course—but awake and this was huge! Impulsivity is one of the symptoms of a brain injury, so they needed to calm him down until they could remove some of the many attachments he had. The doctors and nurses had never seen anything like this before, especially in the ICU. Most of the time, healing from a brain injury is a slow process. But waking up and trying to get out of bed? This was our first sign that Spencer would defy the odds.

The next morning Spencer was moved out of ICU and into a room right next to his brother Jordan. Spencer's room was kept very dark and quiet with no stimuli in accordance with his brain injury. When he woke up for a few minutes at a time, we seemed to see a totally different little boy than who he was before the accident. The staff assured us that this was due to the brain injury, which causes everything—emotions, fears, happiness, anger—to be exaggerated one thousand times. We were completely thrilled that he was still with us, but we also began to realize the work ahead of us.

Five days after the accident, both boys were transferred to a rehabilitation hospital where they shared a room and would begin the long process of getting their strength and skills back. They wanted Spencer up and walking within a few days because he'd been in bed for such a long time. He was in a neck brace, yet with the help of two physical therapists he took his first steps. One therapist held onto a belt around his waist to prevent him from falling while another walked behind him to prevent falls. He wasn't really walking on his own because the therapist was holding him up, but his legs were moving as he tilted to the left like someone who had had too much to drink. Tears rolled down my face as I watched my lively, warm son struggle to take a step.

Yes, I had my son. But was he ever going to be the boy I remembered? What was happening with him? How much work was this going to take? Did I have the stamina? Could I take on his care as well as Jordan's as we moved through the grief of losing their siblings?

You're probably thinking as you read this, just as I did as I wrote it, about how selfish I sound. My boy was injured and I worried about whether I could handle it. I wondered, because I was a mom who had nothing left inside me. I had lost my oldest and youngest children and had another injured boy to worry about and care for. It took everything in me to get up each morning, put on a smile, and "pretend" to my two living children that I was okay and that they would be okay too.

Improvements and struggles

Spencer made huge improvements thanks to intensive therapies, though putting his thoughts into words was difficult. He also didn't seem to have much memory of the events, but would occasionally surprise us. Our biggest surprise was when he half woke up and asked where daddy was. We had been told to tell him the truth but to not include lots of details, which is what I did. He didn't seem to react to my answer, but within a couple of hours we figured out why. He couldn't remember my answer. He asked the same question over and over. It wasn't until later in his recovery that he could remember the answer about his dad.

Spencer slept a lot in his dark and quiet room. When he was overstimulated he would shut down, his brain and body ceasing to function. We soon learned that when this happened he needed to rest. Jordan's rehab was going more quickly. He had some large cuts that had been stitched up, but he was well aware of the accident. Because they were in the same room, Jordan heard his brother ask again and again about their dad and heard the answer repeated again and again. It broke my heart when Jordan asked why his brother wasn't remembering and why he had to hear repeatedly that his dad had died.

Spencer and Jordan were in rehab for two weeks before we headed home and began a regimen of outpatient therapy. Spencer had speech, physical, and occupational therapy four days a week. I brought him to school a few days a week in the morning—the bus ride was too much activity and noise—where he would stay for an hour or so before I picked him up for his therapies or doctor/specialist follow-up appointments an hour away from home.

After our spring break vacation in April, Spencer was able to stay at school longer, making it up to half days by June.

Spencer's first surgery took place in February 2007, a little more than a month after the accident. Surgeons used three mesh plates and screws to repair the orbital bones around his left eye. He didn't lose the sight in that eye, but does have some permanent damage to the optic nerve. Additional surgeries included plastic surgery to repair scars, more eye surgeries, and a dramatic surgery in 2015 to repair his jaw. It lasted six and a half hours and required him to be in the ICU for twenty-four hours and an additional two days in the hospital. There were eight surgeries overall, each one requiring time away from school and more doctor appointments.

Learning and retaining information was difficult for Spencer. I learned what an IEP (Individualized Education

Plan) was, how the school could best accommodate him, and how they would become his advocate. He sometimes had a resource teacher accompany him to regular classrooms but spent the rest of the time in the resource room. He struggled to study, retain information, and take tests. He had to discover what learning style worked best for him, as well as how to advocate for himself as he headed into high school.

Therapies continued for most of Spencer's school years. He lives with headaches daily, and any jarring or loud, repetitive noises have adverse effects. During those early years I had to stop him from doing things that could harm him because he couldn't make good choices due to the impulsivity of TBI sufferers. Now he knows what happens when he doesn't make a good choice and understands the consequences.

There have been lots of tears and frustrations throughout these tough years. I was Spencer's mom first and nurse second. Believe me when I say I know a lot about medical stuff! I was also his chauffeur and his biggest cheerleader. He began this journey as an eight-year-old who cried as he asked me, "Why me? Why did I survive only to have all these things wrong with me? Why am I still here if I can't do anything?"

I answered by asking him to picture a fork in the road. He had two choices when he came to the fork: the way that led to darkness and difficulty or the other path leading to the light. He could choose God's way or Satan's way.

I asked those same questions of myself, as I watched my son struggle and slowly heal. But now, thirteen years after the accident, his progress and life are amazing. Watching others at the hospital or in rehab who had also had TBIs—let me say to God's glory—we all know that Spencer has been blessed beyond words. He is a walking miracle, and God is going to use him for something big.

Jordan, other than his facial scars, came away unscathed. He's also a miracle and very blessed. Someday we hope he will use his story to bless others as well.

The Lord God took the man and put him in the Garden of Eden to work it and take care of it. And the Lord God commanded the man, "You are free to eat from any tree in the garden; but you must not eat from the tree of the knowledge of good and evil, for when you eat from it you will certainly die."—Genesis 2:15–17

Reflection Questions

1. How have you seen God work in your life amid a health crisis?

2. When have you questioned God about the circumstances in your life?

3. How did he answer you? How have your questions changed?

4. When have you experienced a fork in the road that seemed to offer two very different options? Which way did you choose?

5. How has God used your difficult story to bless others? How can you begin talking about your story to help others?

Hope Reflection

A "fork in the road" is symbolic for having to make a decision, much like the Tree of Knowledge of Good and Evil was a symbol in the garden of Eden. God has given us the freedom to make choices in our lives, and sadly, too often we made the wrong ones. Our wrong choices can cause pain and suffering, but they can also help us learn and grow toward making better choices in the future.

We are rewarded for choosing to obey, and reap the consequences for choosing to disobey. I have taught this process to my children starting when they were very young because it's never too early to begin understanding that choices have consequences. Even today, I face the "fork in the road" time and again. I face choosing God's way and choosing another way. It can be a hard choice even when I know God's way is best. Don't doubt his way!

Journal

_____

_____

_____

_____

_____

_____

_____

_____

_____

_____

_____

_____

_____

_____

_____

_____

_____

_____

_____

_____

_____

_____

Prayer

Lord, please guide us when we reach those points in our lives when we have to decide whether we are going to open ourselves to you or close that door. We know that there will be pain in life, but we also know that you are the ultimate healer of our wounds. In Jesus' name, Amen.

CHAPTER NINE

Hearing the Voice of God

"Deep grief sometimes is almost like a specific location,
a coordinate on a map of time. When you are standing
in that forest of sorrow, you cannot imagine that you
could ever find your way to a better place.
But if someone can assure you that they themselves
have stood in that same place, and now have moved on,
sometimes this will bring hope."

—ELIZABETH GILBERT

I had, and continue to have, a lot of conversations with
God as I kneel at my bedroom window. This started
I sought God during my divorce and is now something I
can't do without. One day about a year after the accident,
I poured out my heart to God at my window. I clearly heard
God tell me that Dave and I would have more children
and he emphasized the number three. Plus he gave me a
specific picture of what these children would look like.

What was the significance of that number, I wondered?
And how were we supposed to have more children when

both of us had taken measure to *not* have more? Was God joking, or had I heard something that wasn't there? I shared these details with Dave later that night and he was as shocked as I was. Did I hear what I wanted to hear or was God really talking to me?

I knew in my heart that I couldn't replace the children I lost by having more babies, but that is exactly what I wanted. I wanted more kids. The seed of hope God planted in me that day was part of my healing process as Dave and I began thinking about what more children might look like. I confess my husband wasn't jumping on board with it as quickly as I was, but after prayer and careful consideration, we decided to try in vitro fertilization (IVF). This seemed like the only way we could have our own child.

As we were researching options for adding children to our family, especially after the first two IVFs failed, we dipped our toes into adoption. We filled out an application at a local agency and went in for an interview, but walked away unimpressed. We were told that we only "qualified" for one country should we want an international adoption because Dave was in his mid forties, we already had five children, and we had been married for less than five years. Most countries, the adoption worker told us, were pretty strict with their criteria.

We took it a little further and filled out more paperwork, which I dropped off at the agency. While there I asked about domestic adoption. "Oh no," she said. "You

have too many kids, no one is going to pick you." Seriously?
I walked out to the car and started crying. I called Dave
and told him we couldn't do this anymore, that this wasn't
the way we were supposed to go. That door slamming in
our face had us attempting one more IVF.

After our third IVF attempt in July 2009, we were
pregnant! God was right; I did hear him speak to me about
more children, we obeyed him, and now we were having a
baby. We couldn't believe this was happening to us. I was
thirty-nine and Dave was forty-five and we had had seven
children between us. We were as excited as if this were our
first baby. Which in a way, it was, because it was our first
baby together.

We went in for a ten-week ultrasound and got to see
our baby for the first time. Everything was looking great.
I had always loved being pregnant, but this time it was so
special to be sharing the experience with Dave.

Two weeks later I was volunteering at a local nursing
home doing hair for some of the residents. I felt a little
cramping, but brushed it off to my being older and having
been pregnant six times before (I had had two miscarriages
during the years I was having my four children). More
cramping ensued, and by the time I got home in the early
afternoon I noticed some spotting. The nurse suggested
that I rest, that maybe I'd been on my feet too much.
So I laid down. But within an hour I was having severe
cramping and there was more blood. I was miscarrying.

The two previous miscarriages had been fairly routine as these things go (though losing a pregnancy is never routine), but this time it definitely wasn't routine. There was so much blood! Dave's mom drove me to the hospital, with Dave meeting us there. They did an ultrasound to confirm the miscarriage and kept me there for a while to make sure I didn't need a transfusion because I'd lost so much blood.

I didn't need a transfusion, and we arrived home later that evening. I wanted to curl up in a ball and feel sorry for myself for just a little bit. The little bit lasted a couple of weeks. I couldn't believe that I'd misheard God speaking to me. It had been so real, but I felt like God kept hurting me. Yet I knew that God doesn't randomly hurt or punish his children. We live in a broken world with many difficult heartaches, as I well knew.

I was two weeks away from the miscarriage when Dave called one afternoon. He told me he had heard a commercial on the radio from a different adoption agency. It was having an educational event for people interested in adoption. He told me he felt a prompting that we needed to call and get more information and asked if I would please call. I immediately answered with a great big "No!" I was not going to put myself out there one more time to be hurt *again*. I wasn't sure I could be the positive person I once was.

We decided to agree to disagree on our next step, but I told Dave I would call if only for him, not me. Of course, the first thing he asked when he got home from work that night was whether I had called. I had not. I wanted him to understand that I couldn't take any more rejection—failed IVFs, a miscarriage, a bad experience with an adoption agency. He held me tight and said, "Honey, I believe we have to do this. Will you please do it for me?"

The next day I marshalled my courage and "obeyed" my husband, not with a cheerful attitude but with a sarcastic one. I talked to the sweetest woman, who seemed unfazed by my negativity: "I know we can't do this, and I know we can't do that. So what options do you have for a couple with five kids, married less than five years, and with a husband this old?"

"Have you ever thought about doing a domestic adoption?" she asked.

"Yes, but we were told before that nobody would pick us because we have quite a few kids already," I said.

She quickly answered, "Oh, that's not true. Are you open to different races, by chance?"

When I answered, "Of course we are," everything changed. My heart softened, my voice softened, and my attitude started doing a big turnaround. We set up a meeting with her for a couple of days later, and we were off and running.

We were about six weeks beyond the miscarriage, and doors were flying open. We met with the Adoption Specialist and decided to start the process of adoption, looking at a time frame of possibly nine to twelve months.

There was a lot of paperwork, which was no big surprise, some of which we started right then and some of which we brought home. We also needed to take an adoption class offered by the agency. There was one that very night, or we could wait until next month. We chose that night!

We got to the class and the worker asked our names. When we told her, she pulled us to the side and asked if she might share something with us. Neither of us knew her, and she didn't even look familiar. Yet she told us she had been praying for us; she and her family attended my previous church, though I didn't know her because the church was so large. She knew our story and had been lifting us up to God. How is that not God's hand at work? She was praying for us as I was questioning who and what God is. That's how big God is, caring for little me so much.

The adoption process—with its paperwork, home visits, and requirements—seemed so overwhelming. We dove right in, checking off things as fast as we could and moving on without a hitch. By the second week of January 2010, we were finished and the paperwork was being sent off to the State of Michigan for approval. All we needed was our last home visit.

As January 15 approached, I wondered if the day would take on a different meaning other than "the accident day." Would it be the day we heard news about an adoption? And what was the number three all about? The day came and went, marked in my memory, of course, but no word on the adoption process.

On January 20, 2010, the phone rang in the late morning. It was our adoption agency calling to say our paperwork was approved and that we needed to schedule our last home visit. No way! This was *the* phone call to tell us that a baby boy had been born that morning and his mother had chosen us to parent her child. I could have fallen to the ground in surprise, but I didn't because I was so excited. The older kids had no school that day so Dave was out in the barn with them. I raced to the barn with the news that Grayson David had been born. This adoption was really happening!

We were thinking nine to twelve months, not two and a half months. We needed to go shopping! Car seat, clothes, diapers, bottles, formula, blankets: how would we remember it all? Our heads were spinning as we rushed through the stores and filled the car with baby things. On our way home, my phone rang. It was Dave's mom, who said, "Jamie, I know what the number three means!" I didn't understand.

"The funeral for Zachary and Emma was on January 20, 2007. This is January 20, 2010, and it's a new birth exactly three years to the day after their burials," she said.

Talk about a full circle of life. Life had been taken from me, but new life was given to me exactly how God said it would, not how I thought it should. It's these glimmers of hope that continue to help me on my journey. If I hadn't been able to take those steps with help from others, God, and my husband, I wouldn't have come to recognize the greatness of the God we serve.

> *So do not fear, for I am with you;*
> > *do not be dismayed, for I am your God.*
> *I will strengthen you and help you;*
> > *I will uphold you with my righteous right hand.*
> —Isaiah 41:10

Reflection Questions

1. How have your plans been changed by God throughout the years?

2. How have God's plans been better than what you hoped and dreamed?

3. When have you questioned God's plans for your life? How did you feel as you questioned him?

4. How has God used other people to help you understand him and his plans better?

5. When has God surprised you?

Hope Reflection

My life is, as I'm sure yours is, filled with unexpected events, inconveniences, and interruptions. Haven't we looked forward to a special vacation or night out with friends, only to have it canceled because of a sick child or other crisis? Or a much-needed time with your spouse—after weeks of heading in different directions—gets interrupted by a call from a coworker or the boss? The normal reaction is frustration or anger, and it's easy to throw yourself a pity party.

The reality is that we all have interruptions in our lives; some make the headlines of the news and some are suffered in quiet obscurity. These interruptions, however, are divinely placed on the journey. Each one—based on how we handle it—can be an opportunity to mold us to be more like Christ if we take time to listen and learn.

Journal

_____

_____

_____

_____

_____

_____

_____

_____

_____

_____

_____

_____

_____

_____

_____

_____

_____

_____

_____

_____

_____

_____

Prayer

Father God, we know that through the interruptions of life, both good and not so good, we are given opportunities to rely on you, obey you, and bring you glory in everything. Give us the strength to do just that. In Jesus' name, Amen.

CHAPTER TEN

Following God's Signals

"God's mercy and grace give me hope—
for myself, and for our world."

—BILLY GRAHAM

oing forward we were a family of eight, with children ranging from newborn to age seventeen. The older children adored Grayson and were delighted to have him as part of our family. They had been on board with the adoption from the start. For his part, he adored all of them as well, doing his baby stuff alongside whatever was going on around the house. He attended sporting events, church events, and visited the barn with Dave and the kids.

Yet I couldn't get that number "three" out of my head. God had specifically said "three," and I began to wonder what that might look like. When Grayson was about six months old, I asked Dave about more children. If we decided to go ahead, would we ever consider doing foster care as a route to adoption?

He said, quite boldly in my opinion, that foster care was not on his radar *at all* and that six children, after all, is a lot. I took this to mean that God has blessed us with six, so let's not put ourselves out there via foster care to potentially get hurt again. A part of me couldn't have agreed more, yet a fire had been lit inside me for kids in the foster care system.

My son had an away basketball game that Dave couldn't make until close to the end. As any parent with small children in a huge gym knows, half time is for running around in the hallways. I took Grayson for his halftime run and met a man also letting his children run the hallways.

He asked me if we had adopted Grayson (he's African-American) or if we were doing foster care. I told him we had adopted our son as an infant and what a blessing to our family he has been, and I asked him the same thing. His two children had come to them via foster care first then were adopted into the family. He described what a great experience it had been for his family, and shared a little more about how many children are in foster care and the huge need for families to step forward to help.

I walked back into the gym with Gray to watch the rest of the game. I was feeling more impressed about foster care, but when Dave arrived and I told him the story, he wasn't feeling it like I was. But that encounter prompted me to start investigating foster care on my own to find out more about it and the options and agencies in our area. I got a bit of basic information and left it at that.

We ran into the same man at basketball camp that winter (our sons are the same age), saying hello, asking how it was going, and moving on. This chance meeting didn't feel like chance at all; it felt intentional, as if God was trying to reignite the fire that had started months ago. I truly felt a leaning toward foster care, but I tried to put out that fire, since my husband wasn't on board, and just to keep my life comfortable.

Each Spring Break we head to Florida and this year wasn't any different. In fact, we stayed at the same condo complex we'd stayed at the year before. We were there with friends who stayed with their families in nearby condos, so one evening we visited them for a cookout. Dave and our friend were grilling so I walked around back with Grayson to see the water. Several other children were playing nearby, so naturally Grayson wandered over to see what was going on. Soon the children's father came out and I explained that the ball the kids were playing with had drawn my son.

He laughed and said, "Do you remember me?"

Here was the man from the basketball game in front of me on a shore in Florida! Here was the man who had started my interest in foster care. He asked me if we had inquired about foster care and if I had any questions. I was so stunned that the only question I could come up with was to again ask the name of the agency he had worked with. He ran into the condo and came back with his business card and the name of the agency written on the back.

How is it that God used this man numerous times to get his point across to me but that every time Dave wasn't with me to talk to him too? I walked back down the beach flying high. Foster care was clearly what God wanted us to do; I felt that conviction strongly, which is how God usually works in me. Nothing subtle for me!

I rushed back in to tell Dave the story and show him the business card. I thought that Dave would rush out to talk to the guy and he would start to feel the same as I did about foster care. I retold the stories of when I'd met this guy, but Dave was unmoved. I started to cry in bed that night, asking Dave why he wasn't budging on foster care when I so clearly had a word from God that this is what we were supposed to be doing. He explained again that he was very happy with the six kids we had. This was hard for me to hear, but I knew that God knew my heart and that God needed to be the one to change Dave's heart. That wasn't my job.

A year later

We were on our way to Florida again a year later in 2012 when I told Dave that if we ran into that man again, it was surely a sign and he wouldn't be able to deny that God had something going on. We didn't, much to my dismay, but on our last day at the pool we started talking to another family with young children. They shared how they were just finishing classes to become foster parents, and how many of their friends had done the same and some had also adopted through foster care. As disappointed as I was, I was fine with how Dave felt. Maybe foster care was my dream only.

On our way home, we discussed the highlights of the trip including meeting that family at the pool. I mentioned how cool it was that they stepped forward to foster and love on those kids (he agreed), and I joked that we didn't see that guy again, so it must be the sign we were waiting for (he was silent). Then he asked about the agency that was always mentioned, but I only knew the name of the agency, nothing more.

"Why are you asking me about that agency," I said.

"Because when we get home I think you need to call," he said, as if he was ordering a hamburger at a drive-thru window.

"What?!"

"I want you to call and get some information. See if their boundaries reach where we live. I guess it doesn't hurt to ask questions," he said calmly.

Who was this person? Of course, I called Monday morning.

After answering a lot of questions, the agency representative told me she'd get back to me within the week with answers to my questions, including whether our house in the country fell within their boundaries for foster homes. I didn't hear anything all week, but on Saturday morning the mail included a large packet of papers from the foster care agency. I wondered if this was a mistake seeing as we hadn't gotten a call back.

Another Monday morning call. The woman who answered didn't know if we lived within the boundaries, but put me on hold to check. She came back on with amazing news: we were within a tenth of a mile of being out of their range in faraway Hamilton. We could indeed be foster parents.

Within a few weeks we were enrolled in the classes required for potential foster care parents. Every possible scenario was discussed even to the point of being scary. A few weeks into the classes, I woke up one morning feeling burdened. I was ready to throw in the towel. Spencer had physical therapy that morning and I needed to take Grayson, then two, with us. Any mom knows that two-year-olds can be a handful, and that morning was one of those days. I couldn't imagine more children added to this crazy life. What had I been thinking?!

I read books to Grayson while Spencer went through his therapy. It wasn't long before the receptionist asked if Grayson was adopted or if we were doing foster care. "How cool," she responded when I told her he was adopted. She then revealed that she and her husband had done foster care for more than twenty years and had adopted several of the children. It was the most rewarding thing she'd done in her life, and now her daughter and son-in-law were taking classes to become foster parents. Turns out we were in the same class!

As if that wasn't enough, a minister was talking on a local Christian radio station on our way home about how his church came around children who had no families. The congregation had given up its building fund to purchase a home for these kids to live in and hired an older couple to act as house parents. He spoke of the love his congregation had for these children and the obligation we have as God's people to care for orphans. I burst into tears!

I had called Dave that morning to say that we weren't pursuing foster care anymore and that we had plenty of children. Here I was, ready to give up our plans because it was too much, when God was revealing that nothing is too big for him to accomplish. I'd changed my mind by the end of the day.

As we prepared for foster care, we decided to go through the home study for adoption in case a foster placement led to adoption. Dave had that random thought during one of our classes. Yes, the husband who wasn't on board to begin with was now wanting to take the process further. This is the husband who has to methodically think about everything and cannot make quick decisions—every decision needs a process. Well, this process led to a miracle.

By December 2012, the training for foster care was complete as was our home study for adoption. We knew it was just a matter of time before we got a placement, and that time came quickly. On Dec. 21, we received a call saying the agency had a unique situation with a sibling group—a brother and sister—who needed to move quickly from their current foster home due to birth family–related issues. Parental rights had already been terminated. This wasn't a foster placement; we were being asked if we would consider adopting these kids permanently. We had twenty-four hours to look through the paperwork.

I made the phone call to Dave. We thought one more child might be in our future, but now possibly two? We asked God for direction and asked the agency for a photo of the kids to go with the descriptions they sent. The paperwork revealed that the reason for termination of rights was neglect, with the parents unable to fulfill the requirements to get their children back.

We prayed about it, talked to the older children, and made our decision: we were adopting these kids! Then the photograph came and I couldn't believe what I saw. These two kids matched exactly the vision I was given at the same time I heard God say the number "three." I saw then what I saw now: a boy and a girl of Hispanic and African-American descent. The picture took my breath away.

Our plan was to transition the siblings to our home after the holiday season; God's plan was to have them in our home before Christmas. Two days before Christmas, we got a call saying the children would come immediately. We had no clothing, diapers, or Christmas presents. Yet we knew that unusual circumstances such as these are all part of God's plan. Surprises aren't surprises to God. He had orchestrated everything.

Matthew, almost four, and Avari, age two, joined our family that holiday season. They were our greatest gift and we were now a family of ten.

What was adding two more children to the six we already had? Chaos anyway, right? This was a whole different ball game, though. The struggles were obvious; our Matthew and Avari were behind in basic skills. Communication was sometimes just grunts; they climbed on the counter tops; they tried to stick things in the outlets: all behaviors curbed early in life, but behaviors they didn't know were wrong. They also had no physical boundaries, walking up to strangers and hugging or sitting on their laps. My heart hurt so much for them in the early days.

We decided quite quickly that I would stay home and start working with them from the beginning. Dave and I were blessed in that I could stay home at this time. In those first months, we concentrated on their speech, play therapy, and boundary issues. They felt like some very long months, but the hard work was worth every second.

I can't imagine not having taken the risk of adoption through foster care. If we don't take risks because we don't want to be uncomfortable, if we never take steps to see what God has for us next, where would any of us be? Stuck in the same place and likely missing out on blessings God could give us. God prepares us, cares for us, and sustains us amid the risks and the uncomfortableness.

But when he, the Spirit of truth, comes, he will guide you into all the truth. He will not speak on his own; he will speak only what he hears, and he will tell you what is yet to come." —John 16:13

Reflection Questions

1. When have you felt led by God toward a particular path or decision?

2. How did it feel when others didn't feel that same call?

3. What signposts have you seen in your life that you felt were God's leading?

4. What risks have you taken? How has God been by your side during those risky times?

5. What surprises has God brought into your life? How did those surprises make you feel?

Hope Reflection

When God sent a word to me about us having more children, I decided to be more intentional with my prayers. I needed to find out if this desire was my heart speaking after my loss or if it was truly a message from God. This path was not one I could have come up with on my own, yet it has clearly been for our good and God's glory.

When Dave or I weren't feeling strong enough to keep following God's lead, the other of us was given the strength to step up and carry the burden so we could both carry on. This path, especially regarding children, was clearly orchestrated by God and we were blessed when we followed him. God is so good!

Journal

_____

_____

_____

_____

_____

_____

_____

_____

_____

_____

_____

_____

_____

_____

_____

_____

_____

_____

_____

_____

Prayer

Thank you, God, for knowing my heart better than I do. I wouldn't be the person I am today without hearing your word so boldly. I humbly come before you, asking for you to continue to bless the direction that you have for my life. Guide my steps, Lord. In Jesus' name, Amen.

CHAPTER ELEVEN

Glimmers of Hope

"Hope is not the conviction that something will turn out well but the certainty that something makes sense, regardless of how it turns out."

—VACLAV HAVEL

As I worked on the narrative of this book, I remembered so much about those difficult days surrounding the accident. But finishing the story didn't stop the memories from coming. Sometimes they came in quick snapshots, sometimes in long-running scenes. Let me share a few of these thoughts and memories.

Right after the accident, I was asked to identify my son Zachary's body. I didn't even have to think about it. No, I wasn't going to because I didn't want that memory to be the last one I had of my son. Curt's brother stepped in and identified Zach.

As they wheeled Emma's body away to harvest her organs, I knew it would be the last time I heard her heartbeat, felt her warmth, saw her face. I wanted so badly for the doctors to be wrong, I ached for a miracle and that she would live. But there was no miracle. We were saying good-bye to her forever. I still remember seeing her pink-painted fingernails and toenails. I wanted time to stop for me and my baby girl.

I didn't want to figure out the details for the visitation and funerals. I didn't care what kind of music would be played, who would talk, and simply just didn't care about the big or small details. But I had to pick out two caskets. As I walked in to look at caskets, my knees buckled and my legs fell out from underneath me. The same thing had happened when I walked into Jordan's hospital room. Was this really happening? I felt like I was living in a movie because these things don't happen in real life, do they?

Jordan was allowed to attend the visitation for a few minutes before everyone arrived. The doctor allowed this because Jordan knew what had happened, but she didn't want Jordan exposed to germs and a lot of people because of the high possibility of infection. A good friend picked him up from the hospital and brought him to the church. I saw my bruised and battered son step out of the car and get into his wheelchair. He looked so frail. We wheeled him to each of the three caskets—his dad, his brother, and his sister—and he said his good-byes. My heart ached for both of us.

The number of people who came to the visitation at the church was remarkable. The line of people filled the hallway and went out the door. Friends past and present, classmates, teachers old and new, neighbors, people I hadn't seen for years—all there to show their love for us. People told us they didn't know what to say, and that was fine. Just being there was enough and the hugs spoke the loudest. By the end of the night my chin was rubbed raw from all the hugging. A bit of advice for those with friends or family experiencing a tragedy: There isn't one word that can take the pain away, but a good hug helps.

Jordan and Zach shared a bedroom, so Jordan was faced right away with the emptiness of the bed next to him. I could hardly stand to look at Zach's stuff so I left it the way it was, until a few months later when Jordan asked if we could clean out Zach's side of the room. My first thought was to wonder how he dared ask such a thing so soon, but then I realized it wasn't about me. I needed to do what Jordan needed.

We had gone to a Hamilton varsity basketball game a few days before the accident. Emma always had a bag of toys and snacks she brought with her as she made her rounds to friends sitting around us. That bag was still in her locker at our home, as well as her pink Barbie school backpack and the pair of shoes she'd left out. I couldn't touch those things, or anything of hers. I think I was afraid I wouldn't remember her. It's as if I wanted life to stand still with her still in it; my life, after all, had stopped. Why was everyone and everything else returning to normal?

Dave wanted to go to another basketball game a few weeks after Zach's and Emma's passing, but I couldn't be around people or pretend to be happy. He went to the game and I decided to run to Target. Target is a happy place, right? It was my first time driving after the accident and I made sure not to drive down the same road where my babies had died. In fact, I vowed never to drive down that road again! Emma and I had gone to Target often, enjoying our lunches there. When I walked in the door, the café area was my first reminder of happier days, so I rushed past only to encounter the girls' clothing department. I started crying, hoping that if I walked on I would be okay.

But my body froze. I started to panic and couldn't move. I was a complete mess as I had what I thought was the beginning of a panic attack. I did the only thing I could do: I called Dave, my rock. He instantly calmed me down and talked me all the way home. I had purchased nothing, but I got home in one piece. I was facing a new normal, with every young man resembling Zach making me look twice and every little girl with blonde hair or a bubbly personality drawing my long stare. There were doubles of them everywhere, I thought. But maybe I just longed to see the faces of my children again.

When I went to the grocery store, I saw people trying to "hide" because they didn't know what to say to me, which I understood, as well as those who stopped and had a conversation out of kindness. One time someone commented that I was looking really good. I wanted to say thank you, but was confused because I knew my heart and thoughts were hidden and certainly didn't look good! If people could have seen my heart, they would have known I was dying. Plain and simple, just trying to exist was difficult. Some days I would have loved for someone to ask me how I was doing, and other days I just wanted to disappear.

I used to sit in my bathtub trying to drown out my crying, or I'd read a book that might help me understand the things I was experiencing. I received a lot of books at the beginning so I was reading all the time. Some books were quite good, others not so helpful. Reading helped occupy time when I was alone and helped me understand I wasn't losing my mind as much as I thought I was. I just wanted answers. I learned that the brain cannot process trauma; it just spins as the brain searches for solid answers, but there are no answers with trauma because it doesn't make sense.

I went through every stage of grief. One book said that I needed to experience each stage of grief in exact order to be okay. Needless to say, I didn't finish that book. All I needed was for someone to tell me I wasn't losing my mind.

Anger was a tough stage to work through. Every stage was, but anger seemed to be the hardest for me. I was very angry at God, Curt, the truck driver, and life in general. I chose to look back and dwell on every single detail, which wasn't helpful at all. In one of my crying rages, Dave grabbed hold of me and asked why I wanted to relive every detail and whether it helped at all. He wanted to know if we could go back and change the details (no, of course not) and whether we could do anything about any of it.

"God says he's so big and knows every hair on our head," I cried. "Why did he allow this to happen to me?"

"God doesn't always stop things from happening, Jamie," Dave answered. "It's the fallen world we live in that began with Adam and Eve. God cries when you do, he hurts because you hurt. He doesn't choose to hurt you by taking away things you love."

"Well, that doesn't help me make sense of it all," I said.

"It was an accident. It doesn't make sense. Things just happen! God doesn't cause accidents; accidents happen because of choices," he said.

I'm not saying the semi driver chose to pull out because he wanted to kill three people and to injure two others. Maybe he didn't take a second look before pulling out, or maybe he kept rolling for better momentum in the snowy weather. We all make choices to keep our lives more comfortable and sometimes accidents happen. I could be angry at Curt for not having my four-year-old in a proper car seat, but that was his choice and not mine. My eight-year-old and ten-year-old could have been in seat belts, as they should have been, but were laying down instead. We all make choices daily, but it's only when things go wrong that we look back and want things to be different. I chose not to be bitter and angry with the truck driver. What he had to live with for the rest of his life was punishment enough, so who was I to make him suffer more. He would have to answer for his motives and feelings, not me.

It's easy to stay bitter and angry. It's the place Satan wants you to stay, the place he can come in to destroy. It's harder to choose peace and love, but isn't that what Jesus did for us? Can you imagine choosing to be crucified so that others may be saved? I'm not comparing my situation to Jesus being nailed to a cross, but it's a visual we can use to be reminded of our choices.

My counselor, a Christian, offered me a visual I have never forgotten. She asked me to picture myself entering the tomb as Jesus did: bloody, beaten, dead, wrapped in strips of linen. Then Jesus came back to life and those strips were laid on the ground. Imagine, she said, that each strip falling away signifies something you need to leave behind to have life again. This was such a beautiful picture and so freeing to "peel off" strips that had held me so long. There were some things I held onto and would need to peel off later, but with the removal of each one, I was able to live more freely than I could have imagined.

Before you search for the right counselor, it's important to investigate. You'll know after the first session whether the counselor is the right fit for you. A good counselor is critical for people who have experienced any sort of trauma. That person can equip you with coping mechanisms and help you take steps to continuing moving forward. Counseling was a huge part of my life in dealing with my divorce, learning who I was, and then dealing with my loss. God put me with the people I needed at the times I needed them most.

I cleaned out Zachary's closet because Jordan asked me to and I felt it was part of Jordan's healing process. It was a hard step because I had placed so much value in my kids' belongings. I idolized their stuff in a way. I couldn't fathom washing their sheets ever again because I might forget their special scent. I finally figured out that the value I placed on their things was about me not wanting to forget anything about them. Never touching or moving anything doesn't bring them back or replace the loss; it kept me stuck in time.

No one touched Emma's pink room—her favorite color of course—for a year and a half after the accident. It was a corner room that I never had reason to enter. I could see the four stuffed animals she slept with, her pajamas on top of her dresser. Everything was exactly as she left it the final time she left our home. I could hardly walk in, much less clean, her room. I knew I should but each time I tried I walked back out sobbing.

Then one day I got a call from a friend's husband asking if he could stop by on his way home from work. Jon told me he had a story to share. When he got to our house, he told me this: Two nights prior, he had woken when he thought his wife had turned on the lamp. When he looked around, instead of seeing the lamp, he saw Emma standing there surrounded by light. "Tell my Mommy I'm okay," she said, and immediately the light was gone.

He struggled for a couple of days about telling me, afraid he'd sound weird or that I wouldn't believe him. I totally believed him! His experience sounded similar to what I had experienced with Zach. His experience was exactly what I needed to hear, and God knew I needed to hear it from someone I would least expect. Jon will tell you to this day that seeing Emma changed his life forever. That same week, with help from my dear friend Lynae, I cleaned out Emma's closet. That confirmation that she was okay allowed me to move forward.

A few months after the accident, my neighbor Jean called out of the blue and asked if I'd like to attend a Bible study with her and a few other ladies. Jean and I had talked a few times before, but hadn't interacted beyond our front yards. Was I ready for something like this with people I didn't know? The group met in the home of a woman who had been bedridden with an unexplainable diagnosis.

She had severe muscle spasms and was in constant pain. She laid in a hospital bed twenty-four hours a day. Our chairs formed a half circle around her bed, which faced the living room window. She showed such amazing joy for life and love for God. I couldn't imagine lying in bed all day, writhing in pain, and still having such abounding joy. If she could find joy in her circumstances, then I could too. I found hope in seeing that glow from the light shining through the window onto that woman in pain.

When I asked Jean later why she invited me to that Bible study, she said, "I asked the Lord what I could do to help you, and he told me I needed to invite you." She did as she was prompted. All the negative energy I put into talking myself out of going was rewarded tenfold, thanks to the blessings these godly women poured into me.

Our group met for several years, eventually dissolving because of work and life schedules. I later learned that my bedridden friend attended a healing ceremony performed by a man from Kenya. Her body was healed completely, and today she walks and moves as if those years of being bedridden never happened.

These vignettes may seem random, but to me they represent glimmers of hope. Those glimmers came from family and friends who helped us through the darkest days, from strangers, and from my sweet Emma herself. It is this hope, this heart of God, that brings me joy each day.

Why, my soul, are you downcast?
Why so disturbed within me?
Put your hope in God,
for I will yet praise him,
my Savior and my God.
—Psalm 43:5

Reflection Questions

1. What decisions have you made regarding end-of-life issues such as palliative care and organ donation? List and set action steps for these issues.

2. What value do you place on "things"? How are you holding onto things instead of facing your pain?

3. When have you heard God speaking to you? Did you act on those words or ignore them?

4. How have others come alongside you in your difficult times? How have you come alongside others?

5. Describe some of the "glimmers of hope" you've seen in your dark days.

Hope Reflection

When I was faced with the question about donating my daughter's organs, as hard as it was, I never considered saying no. I could have played the victim, or said, "My daughter is gone; why would I want to give life to someone else?" But I chose not to. Months later, when I received letters from some of the recipients, I didn't feel joy. It hurt to my core to hear how thrilled they were to have life given back to them. Of course, I was happy for them, but it felt like my life had stopped with the deaths of my daughter and son.

Today, I have found joy and I wouldn't change my decision for anything. I am thrilled to know that my little princess was able to give life to so many. I feel like her sparkly personality, which God gave her, is somehow planting little seeds of Jesus into those recipients. Despite the awful circumstances, God found a way to give life.

Journal

_____

_____

_____

_____

_____

_____

_____

_____

_____

_____

_____

_____

_____

_____

_____

_____

_____

_____

_____

_____

_____

_____

Prayer

Heavenly Father, we become so focused on our own needs that we forget about others who are sick or suffering. It's not that I don't care about them; I just need you to strengthen me to give when I don't feel like it. Teach me to embrace my choices as part of my spiritual growth, and help to make the best choices. When I see myself as you do, I can help others more easily. In Jesus' name, Amen.

CHAPTER TWELVE

A Legacy of Hope

"But I know, somehow, that only when it is dark enough can you see the stars."

—MARTIN LUTHER KING, JR.

M y life is and always will be a work in progress. I don't ever want to be "comfortable" because I want to live life intentionally and with purpose. I feel like that's why I've gone through the things I have. I've come out on the other side a different person, a person I wouldn't have been had I not faced these trials. If I didn't believe in the hope of Jesus, I would be a lost soul.

As a fitting end to this book, I asked our five oldest children—the Fab Five as they call themselves—a few questions about our lives before and after the accident. I asked them to be as honest and raw as they wanted to be and promised to not question anything they wrote or tell the others what they wrote. Each one is seeing for the first time what the others had to say.

My questions to them were:

1. How do you feel the blending of our families went then and now?

2. What was the feeling in our home before, during, and after the accident?

3. What are things we as parents have instilled in you?

4. What legacy has been left to you through these events?

These are deep questions about circumstances unique to our family. Though you may never face the same trials, I pray that what we have learned may encourage your hearts. Our kids faced a lot of adversity when they were young, at a time when most kids were consumed with thoughts of clothing, hair styles, social media, and teenage crushes. Our children faced some huge life decisions, and came through the better for making those decisions well.

Collin, now twenty-three, is Dave's youngest child and second oldest of the five boys. He was six years old when Dave and I met, nine at the time of the accident.

Blending families: I loved it. It was an exciting time knowing I was going to have three brothers, especially because of having two older sisters. I always wanted brothers and a younger sister. I wasn't going to be the youngest anymore.

At home: The feeling in our home before the accident was exciting. I remember when we were building the house; we would go over on weeknights and weekends to make race tracks for our bikes and quad. We talked about getting to share rooms and how exciting it was going to be.

After the accident: There was a void in all of us. I remember that time as if it was yesterday. The morning of the accident, Jamie and I were sitting in the lockers [we use for storage] waiting for the boys and Emma to arrive. I said, half joking, that maybe they had gotten in an accident on their way home, though I'm not sure why and what made me think that. I was in shock when I got called down to the school office after the first recess and saw my mom and two sisters there. I knew it wasn't good.

I think a piece of us is still missing. My big brother Zach was taken from us. I remember that whenever we played football or basketball in the backyard, it was always Zach and I against Jordan and Spencer. I looked up to Zach so it was tough to grasp the reality that I wouldn't see him and Emma again until it was my time to go be with them.

Instilled in us: Both parents have instilled in us the value of having a positive attitude about everything we do. The biggest thing is that we get to choose our attitude and embrace it every day. I don't think you'll find many families that have been through what we have that still have good attitudes like we do. It would have been easy for Jordan and Spencer to have bad attitudes and say that life had given them a bad hand, but they don't. It would have been easy for Jamie to say that God was out to get her, to ask why God had taken her two children. But she didn't. I know it wasn't always easy, but my parents' attitudes taught me how to respond well and about what's really important.

Legacy: Many people think a legacy is about money, but a legacy is far more than that. Your legacy is about life lessons, values, and how you've been taught to think. We can pass that down to our own kids. I think the biggest legacy we received was teaching us that when adversity comes, our response is so important. We were also taught to be kind to others because we don't know what they're going through. Most importantly, be a godly person who serves others, be the good in the world, and realize the impact we have on others' lives.

I think about the three "littles" and where they would be without a family who loves them unconditionally. It's amazing that Brandi and Austin are following God's prompting in their hearts to venture into foster care, following in our parent's footsteps, and it motivates me to do the same thing, to have an impact on someone's life like you have done for us.

I also hope to build on the legacy of the Zach Boeve Memorial Basketball Court at school. The big reason I wore Zach's jersey number 42 while playing basketball was because I knew how much Zach loved the sport, and wearing that number reminded me every time I took the court to not take life for granted because we are on earth for only a flicker. What am I going to make of that flicker?

Alexandra, now twenty-eight, is newly married to Jedidiah. She is the oldest daughter of Dave and the oldest of the eight children. She was twelve when we met and fifteen at the time of the accident.

I always felt safe and secure. I was always protected by my family and knew what to expect. Home was a haven; it felt like a homecoming when we were all together, with no difference between the last names Tidd and Boeve. I'm not sure how to put that feeling into words, except that it was like I forgot what life was like before and I didn't know anything different except our blended family. Our home felt happy and full.

I felt like a piece of our home also died. I distinctly remember our table feeling empty forever, until I physically got used to seven chairs being filled instead of nine. Our home was quiet, which wasn't normal. It felt uncomfortable because the comfort and security I had known wasn't there anymore. I don't do well with change in an instant. What I thought was secure and steady had just been rocked.

It felt like we couldn't be happy because everything around us was somber all the time. It felt a little like we were on eggshells because we didn't want to do anything that would make anyone upset, no matter how small it was. It felt like we turned into the protectors in some ways because we hated to see Jamie hurt. When we went to Florida for Spring Break, it was like we had a bit of normal back. We were in close proximity to each other and that felt like the first step for our family's healing together. We saw Jamie and Dad happy again and, in turn, it was like we were given the okay to be happy.

I can't put a time frame on "after" because it's hard to nail down when "after" was. I think we started to move into a new normal when Grayson was adopted. We weren't holding on to the past, but Gray helped us move forward. The safety and security slowly came back and we could be comforted in that we were all healing. Currently, I think we have a lot of security in one another that most families don't have. Our home feels full of life again. Our family has transformed. I think the pieces that made up our family before the accident are still true, but now in different shapes.

Our parents have instilled in us the value of hard work, dedication, faith, understanding that the world is bigger than ourselves, and this means that we can be the hands and feet of Jesus.

I think we will always cherish family in a way we wouldn't have before the accident. We will all take that into our own families. We will always cherish and remember family with Zach and Emma, while also recognizing how the accident led to our family as it is now.

Jordan is twenty-four now, my second oldest son, and our oldest boy. He's number three of the eight. He was eight years old when Dave and I met and ten at the time of the accident.

I felt like the blending of our families went easily and smoothly. From the first time I met my step siblings, we were instantly friends. Collin was great; it was like having another brother who loved to do the exact things we did. Both of the girls were great too, and we became really close so fast that it seemed like it happened overnight. Both families went back and forth between separate homes, but every time we hung out together it was like getting to hang out with our friends.

Tragedy shakes everything up. When you already have a blended family, it might seem like it would be tougher to keep everyone together, but it wasn't. Being broken created a unique bond that many can't relate to. I've never believed one of us hurt more than the others because we all lost someone we loved, plus we all saw that loss from different viewpoints.

I don't think our parents had to teach us anything because they showed it to us. They showed us how strength and faith go hand in hand, how love isn't fair but rather an emotion developed through trials. And how joy can turn dark into light.

Leaving a legacy means leaving behind a part of you when you go that others will remember. Selflessness is a quality that may not be rewarded, but it's the most rewarding. That's the legacy my parents will leave.

Spencer, now twenty-two, is number five in the line of eight. He was five when Dave and I met, eight at the time of the accident.

I don't have any memories of how the blending of our family went. I lost all of my past in the accident. It hurts to look at pictures of my dad, brother, and little sister and not remember a thing. It took me a long time to admit I couldn't remember because I didn't want to hurt my mom after all she'd already been through. Our family and what we have is amazing because we are all so close, nobody fights, and everyone would think we are biological brothers and sisters.

I don't have memories of before, during, or after the accident. I can recall a few things here and there if something is brought up, but almost everything is a blur unless it was something pretty big. When I had bad days, I remember my mom describing the choices I could make. As hard as it was and still is at times, I choose the "harder path" and remember the reward of that in the end.

Loyalty, faith, and family first has been instilled in us. All of us have huge hearts and we look out for each other. My parents adopted three kids into our family, showing me a side of what being unselfish means. I hope to one day show that as well. As I work with youth group kids at our church, I am getting to use some of the gifts instilled in me!

The biggest legacy from our parents is their work ethic. Everything takes a lot of hard work and effort if you want what you do to be good. We've all followed that example in what we do and have accomplished, and I hope to pass that on to my kids someday.

Brandi is twenty-six and has been married to Austin for almost two years. She was ten when we met and thirteen at the time of the accident, number two of our eight children. Brandi and Austin are foster parents to a couple of little girls who would steal anyone's heart, especially ours now that we're called Mamie and Poppy.

The first years were instrumental in defining who we were as a family unit. Family priorities were established, with church at the center. As siblings, we meshed. When they say "blended family," it makes me think of a blender. Throw in all different fruits, and after blending it you cannot pick out the different fruits, or separate them. It also wouldn't be as tasty if a few of the ingredients were missing.

Everyone grew close, especially in our tiny rental home. When the house was finally finished, "norms" were established. Summers were awesome. We all had chores and responsibilities, as well as sports, but beyond that, just hanging out together was so much fun. There were so many pickup basketball games, backyard football, and even a time when we were all into Texas Hold 'Em. We played late-night soccer, putting Emma in as goalie. In hindsight that wasn't the brightest idea, but she did it!

When my mom came to school to tell me what happened, I went into a state of disbelief and distanced emotions. We had to go tell Collin at the elementary school, then headed to the hospital. I don't think I chose this, but somehow I felt like I needed to be the one who was "okay." With so much going on and everyone in our family affected in one capacity or another, I just shut down my emotional side. This followed me around for years and negatively impacted a lot of relationships. At the funeral home visitation, I remember feeling numb. I didn't cry. Then Dad came to me and whispered, "She was your little princess." For the first time, I felt something. I hung my head and cried. But I quickly returned to not feeling.

When the boys were in the hospital, there was a shift from grief to hope in the boys' recovery. We spent a lot of hours in the car and at hospitals. Dad kept telling me how hard it was going to be to go back to school, but it actually helped me return to some sort of normalcy. I would often look down at Zach's locker and go into a daze. If a teacher saw me, he or she would quickly call the school counselor and I'd end up in the office, which I hated. Returning to school helped push down my emotions further. Again, I felt like the one who had to be strong and okay.

The first year after the accident was a blur. We all were grieving in our own ways. Some of us processed internally, while others processed externally. My grief presented in withdrawal. Then I'd externalize everything that had been building up and explode, usually at my dad.

We got really close in the few years after the accident. We blended further together, trying our best to lift each other up when someone needed it. We all had hard days. I typically would approach this with joking around, and so would the boys. Laughter and extreme sarcasm became our normal. The feeling in our home turned from "surviving" to "thriving." We weren't just the ones left behind from the accident, but the family that utilized an extreme tragedy to push us closer to Jesus. We were a family on a mission.

My parents taught me that there's always a choice. Life is hard and there are some curveballs that will try to knock you down. And they will sometimes be successful. You can stay down and be consumed by hardship, or you can choose to say, "Not today, Satan," and get up. You'll be bruised, broken, and changed, but you can rise. All in the name of Jesus.

Conclusion

I was overwhelmed by some of the similarities in responses from our children, but also overwhelmed by the love they have for Jesus, each other, those outside our family, and unbelievably, the "job" we've done as parents. I am humbled to hear from our kids how they felt and feel now. Maybe every parent should ask their kids about the good and tough times before it's too late.

Please don't think that this sounds too perfect or that it's fake. It's not. If I had the space to share all of the "ugly" that happened and still does, I'd have to write another book! I heard a Christian speaker recently quote businessman T. Harv Eker in a statement that sums up life for me: "If you are willing to do only what's easy, your life will be hard. But if you are willing to do what's hard, life will be easy." I believe this statement is true and apply it to my life, because life is not easy.

I ask you, are you preparing yourself? Are you ready for whatever circumstances may play out in your life? What choices will you make? Will you take the easy way, filled with blame and anger? Or will you take the hard way of facing your pain and sin and looking to Jesus? God is always patiently waiting for you. When you are ready, so is he.

I choose Jesus and the salvation he brings. I choose hope and joy. I encourage you to choose those things this day, this minute.

But he said to me, "My grace is sufficient for you, for my power is made perfect in weakness." Therefore, I will boast all the more gladly about my weaknesses, so that Christ's power may rest on me. That is why, for Christ's sake, I delight in weaknesses, in insults, in hardships, in persecutions, in difficulties. For when I am weak, then I am strong. —2 Corinthians 12:9–10

Reflection Questions

1. What legacy have your parents left you? Do you find yourself acting like they did in both good and bad ways?

2. What legacy do you believe you are leaving your children, grandchildren, or younger people in your lives? Be honest.

3. What strategies do you use when responding to the hard things in life? Do you blame or withdraw? Do you seek strength in Jesus?

4. What have you learned as you've read this book? What changes will you make in your life as a result of this book?

5. In what areas of your life can you use more hope and joy? How do you feel God leading you toward hope and joy?

Hope Reflection

If we made a list of all the hardships and personal struggles we could face, it would be endless. It's not true that if you are a Christian you won't have any struggles or bad things happen. And when they do, it would be easy to withdraw, blame others, or blame God. But owning those struggles and moving forward—because you can't go back and change anything anyway—is how God calls us to live.

Jesus himself had struggles with loneliness and despair, and he faced an excruciating death on the cross. Jesus never said life would be easy, but he did say he would be with us through all of it. The hope Jesus offers is a gift beyond imagination.

Journal

_____

_____

_____

_____

_____

_____

_____

_____

_____

_____

_____

_____

_____

_____

_____

_____

_____

_____

_____

_____

_____

_____

Prayer

Oh Father, every one of us has struggles and each one's struggles are different. You are the only one who has the power to take devastating circumstances and tragedies and use them for something good. Your timing is perfect and we are never forgotten. Use your power to strengthen my heart as it is lifted to you. In Jesus' name, Amen.

Acknowledgments

First and foremost, thanks and praises to God the Almighty for his showers of blessings as we were in the trenches and as we continue to follow him every day.

Thank you, Michelle, for listening and praying with me about what God was calling me to do. You put Tim Beals into my life, as well as Ann Byle, both of whom believed in me and that this story needed to be told. Without your help, this book would not have happened.

This book is something God laid on my heart sixteen years ago. Never could I have imagined the bigger hurdles that were to come. Because of those hurdles, this story is deeper and more heartfelt. God wrote my story—and all of our stories—and I'm here to share the news of how good God is and to bring hope to those who feel hopeless. It wasn't easy to accept the struggles in my life, but it's even harder to watch others face tough times. I have a fixer heart, so I want to help each one of you not have to struggle as much as I did. I know only God can soothe your pain, but if one word or sentence from me can help trigger you choosing God's way, it's worth everything.

To my husband David. You have had to wear a lot of hats during our marriage, especially in the early years. You are the first to say that those hats weren't always a perfect fit, but you wore them anyway and still do with strength and love. You have been my rock, a shoulder to cry on that I soaked with tears, arms to hold me up when I couldn't hold myself. You have been ears to listen, even in the middle of the night when I couldn't sleep because my brain was swirling. God knew exactly what he was doing putting you in my life. I trusted you back then, not knowing what was coming, and still do. You've taught me what a marriage partnership looks like and I know the best is yet to come. Much love, and thank you!

My boys, where do I begin? Jordan and Spencer, you have had more things happen in your life by the age of ten than most people have in a lifetime. I hope you one day can show your strong faith and perseverance to your own wives and families. To share the adversity you've overcome will only make you and them stronger. You've grown into great men despite losing your dad, whose shoes were filled by Dave teaching you the ropes as any father would. God is writing your story too, so be still and listen. Love always, Mom.

Alex and son-in-law Jed, Brandi and son-in-law Austin, and Collin, I call you my children because you are, though I know you also have your mother. We have had a strong bond since the day we met. We have had some great times as well as some very rough patches, so thank you for your patience and love. That love never wavered, and now I can see as you've gotten older some of the foundations we laid down as a family. My heart is full as I watch you girls in married life and the men you have chosen. Love you, Mames.

Jacob, Grayson, and Avari (the littles): The three of you have brought so much love to our family. You have overflowed our hearts beyond what we could have imagined. There will be struggles in your lives, but you are being equipped now for when they come your way. God has some pretty big things for you, and we thank God for allowing us to be part of your lives. Love you more, Mom.

I lost my dad seven and a half years ago to a sudden heart attack at the age of sixty-seven. I know he would be so proud of me, but better yet is knowing he is in heaven playing with Zach and Emma, getting to love them as a grandpa would. Thanks, Dad.

Thanks to my mom, to my brother—who has always been my protector—to my sister-in-law, and to my nephew. Thanks for always being there and available. What would we do if we didn't have each other?

Thanks to my in-laws for accepting me into the Tidd family. We endured another loss when we lost Dad to a sudden stroke. We miss you, Gramps T. To my sister-in-law, brother-in-law, and niece and nephews, thank you for taking me on as the newbie and going through what we have together.

God has blessed me abundantly with both families and many wonderful friends who have cheered me on through this process. This depth of joy, love, and meaning in life is something I couldn't have dreamed of.

There have been some dark moments. I could have easily given up, but I kept going. Keep going. Your life is not over, and you never know what chapters are to come. Your greatest ones are still ahead. I hope this fire burns inside you as it does me, to know that nothing is ever too broken, too far gone, or too hopeless to be made new again. For that, I am forever grateful.

About the Author

Jamie Tidd and her husband, David, have been married for fifteen years. Together they have eight children and live in a small community in West Michigan. Jamie serves as a shepherding elder at her local church and is developing a speaking ministry around her message of hope. Life's unimaginable tragedies have given her the ability to breathe life back into those she talks to and those who read her words. Her dream is to encourage you, her readers and listeners, to work hard and persevere with God's help as you create your own story.